# TALL BLONDES

## A BOOK ABOUT GIRAFFES

### LYNN SHERR

**Andrews McMeel
Publishing**

Kansas City

Designed by Randall Blair Design.

Library of Congress Cataloging-in-Publication Data
Sherr, Lynn.
     Tall blondes : a book about giraffes / Lynn Sherr.
          p.      cm.
     Includes bibliographical references.
     ISBN 0-8362-2769-7 (hd)
     1. Giraffe—Miscellanea. I. Title
QL737.U56S48 1997                     96-29880
599.638—dc21                         CIP

# Contents

# Acknowledgments

Books, unlike television programs, are the work of a single author. But while the concept and execution (and any mistakes) are mine, I was rarely alone in writing *Tall Blondes*. To everyone who has ever given me a giraffe likeness or tolerated my obsession or simply stood by, thank you. I am especially grateful to the following:

For permission to quote from their works: Mary Ann Hoberman, text © 1991; John Ciardi, text © 1984; Jay Jacobs, © 1981; Johannes Eff, © 1979 by National Review, Inc., 150 East 35th St, N.Y. 10016; Lloyd Shearer, *Parade*; John J. Kinahan.

For their help and guidance in Africa: in Kenya, Bryony and Rick Anderson for taking care of me at Giraffe Manor, and Betty Leslie-Melville for creating it; in South Africa: the rangers and proprietors of Londolozi, Ngala, and Makalali Lodges; in Zimbabwe: Khatshana and Matobo Hills.

For sharing their expertise in the captive animal world: Dale Leeds, Cheyenne Mountain Zoo; Jim Doherty, Kris Theis, and Linda Corcoran at the Wildlife Conservation Society; Margie Gibson, National Zoological Park; Debbie Pearson, Marwell Park Zoo; Karl Kranz, Philadelphia Zoo; Tony Vecchio and Debbie Richmond, Roger Williams Park Zoo; and Dr. Rod East. For my visits to the extraordinary White Oak Conservation Center, a division of Gilman Paper Co.: Howard Gilman, John Lukas, and Natalie Moody (plus Linda Fairstein and Justin Feldman for getting me there).

Roger and Jill Caras have fed my giraffe habit for years. I would also like to thank Ellen Futter, Alex James, and Nina Root of the American Museum of Natural History; Arthur W. Arundel; Natalie Boutin; Richard (Chip) Burkhardt; Matt Carmill; the Dali Museum; Margaret Douglas-Hamilton; Richard Estes; Professor Ahmet Ferhadi; Stephen Jay Gould; Dr. Alan Hargens; Marvin L. Jones; Vernon Kisling; Laura Bingaman Lackey; Professor Bernard Lewis; Dorcas MacClintock; Florence Martin and Mme. Mireille Martin; Ann Medlock; Gerard Middleton; John Polacsek; Richard J. Reynolds; Dr. Nikos Solounias; Dr. Robert Van Citters; the Victor Invictus Society: Kay Partney Lautman and Donal MacLaughlin; and Rosalie Wolff and Dr. Robert Carlucci.

Very personal thanks to my agent and friend Esther Newberg, who has again demonstrated her support and genius; Jean Lowe and her colleagues at Andrews and McMeel, for their enthusiasm and creativity; and the Hilford gang—James and Aline, Andrew and Jeffrey—who have uncomplainingly shared our homes with giraffes.

To Lois Sherr Dubin—travel mate, roommate, soul mate—I dedicate this book.

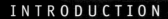

**T**O UNDERSTAND THIS BOOK, YOU should know something about me. First, that I stand five feet eight inches and have (mostly) blond hair. Second, that I went to Africa for the first time in 1973 and fell in love. With giraffes. Not that there was anything wrong with elephants, cheetahs, or even warthogs. But giraffes? They were gorgeous. They were unlikely. They were a dazzling, unexpected revelation: gawky, graceful anomalies; cool, gentle giants dressed in golden, stained-glass coats. They had the longest eyelashes I had ever seen. And when they ran, they seemed to float. I was hooked.

After I came home, a number of people asked which animals I had liked best. "Oh, giraffes," I gushed over and over, ticking off the reasons for my new obsession. Everyone nodded politely, with a "That's nice, dear" indulgence—except for one friend. "Yes, of course," she said, nodding wisely. "Of course. Tall blondes."

My first visit to Giraffe Manor, 1985

My own personal bond notwithstanding, you don't have to be blond to appreciate giraffes. In fact, they come in brunette and redhead versions, too, and even black and white. But whatever the color of their skin, or hide, they are universally enchanting—sunny, wondrous creatures whose preposterous physique has made them well worth looking up to. One trip to a zoo and you realize it is impossible to take a bad photograph of a giraffe. One trip to their homeland and you figure out why. When confronted with humans, they actually pose, staring right back with aloof curiosity, seemingly quite pleased with their spectacular spotted selves. A medieval French encyclopedist concluded that the giraffe seemed "not ignorant of its own beauty as it was endowed with fairer colours than all other beasts." Nearly half a century later, an English naturalist put it more fancifully: "When any come to see them, they willingly and of their own accord turn themselves round as it were of purpose to shew their soft hairs, and beautiful colour, being as it were proud to ravish the eyes of the beholders."

To my mind, giraffes are a stately, serene presence in a tumultuous world. They embody the best and worst in all of us: the awkwardness that inhibits our social lives; the poise that inhabits our dreams. Watch a giraffe splay its legs to take a drink and you will know the true meaning of insecurity. Watch a herd gallop across the savanna and you will grasp the essence of elegance.

But there is more. Meet a giraffe face-to-face and I guarantee you will lose your heart. In 1985, on assignment for ABC news at the U.N. Women's Conference in Nairobi, I had the good fortune to stay just outside the city in a private home-turned-wildlife-center called Giraffe Manor. There, in a great stone mansion surrounded by acres of African bush, I watched, petted, fed, and observed six splendid specimens who had either been raised there or grown tame enough to hang around humans. I gave them cereal and carrots and discovered their eighteen-inch-tongues; I climbed the visitors' platform in the backyard and stared right into their lustrous, melting eyes, each one bigger than the spread of my hand. I petted their sumptuous tawny fur and scratched the hairy horns atop their heads. And sometimes, while eating my own breakfast, I had the giddy pleasure of discovering that a giraffe had poked its head inside the window and over my shoulder for a handout. My husband, who had long since agreed to share our New York apartment with an assortment of wood, clay, metal, and cloth giraffe likenesses, worried that I would never come home when confronted with the real thing.

When I did return and started researching my new alter egos, I realized I had tapped into a rich vein of giraffe lore. Centuries of travelers' diaries, natural histories, and appreciative articles celebrate their singular impact on our lives. Captain William Cornwallis Harris, a British adventurer who is credited with organizing Africa's first hunting safari (in 1836), understood the magic and the fantasy:

> *The colossal height, and apparent disproportions of this extraordinary animal, long classed it with the unicorn and the sphinx of the ancients, and induced a belief that it belonged rather to the group of chimeras with which the regions of imagination are tenanted, than existed amongst the actual works of nature.*
> —*Capt. William Cornwallis Harris, 1844*

Johnson Plane, "The Spirit of Africa"

A reporter for *Frank Leslie's Popular Monthly* wrote in 1878, "In quaintness of exterior, no African beast surpasses the giraffe. . . ." And a zoo curator, facing his first giraffe in the wild, summed it up: "Here stands a creature that symbolizes Africa perhaps more than any other of the Dark Continent's magnificent animals. Nothing like it roams any other part of the world."

Explorers Osa and Martin Johnson, who filmed wildlife in Kenya during the 1920s and 1930s, painted a giraffe-hide pattern on one of their amphibious airplanes and named it "The Spirit of Africa."

More recently, the comely pattern has been painted on an oil rig in Bahrein and construction cranes in Stockholm harbor. Those of us without such colossal forms to decorate have incorporated the giraffe into our lives in more conventional ways. In literature the giraffe symbolizes someone special— someone who either stands out above the crowd or who sticks out like a sore thumb. In her novel *Felix Holt*, George Eliot compares a certain formidable barrister possessing untold powers to the first live giraffe brought to England in 1805: he "was to be contemplated, and not criticised." A children's book, *Giraffes Have More Fun*, translates the animal's unique nature into youngsters' terms. Sally dresses up like a giraffe because "I bet it's more fun than being a little girl." She sees herself winning the high jump, reaching the cookie jar, getting a longer Christmas stocking. But the advantage of Sally's new identity really becomes clear when her mother asks her to straighten up her room. "No, I'm a giraffe," Sally responds. "Giraffes don't have to clean their bedrooms."

Cartoonists have long appreciated the comic possibilities of a tall, thin constitution, and one animated version was nominated for an Academy Award. Not surprisingly, the giraffe world has proven a choice target for Gary Larson, whose deliciously twisted wit manages to make the totally absurd seem utterly rational.

Giraffes have also infiltrated politics, as battlefield tributes (see chapter 1), as valued diplomats (see chapter 7), and as secret messengers of peace during World War II (see chapter 8). There is a giraffe constellation, a series of giraffe money (it is the hidden watermark on paper currency in Tanzania), a

Danish beer, and, the last time I checked, a growing array of sites on the Internet communicating news about giraffes. One cyberartist who calls herself the Digital Giraffe says she picked the name because "giraffes stand tall among their fellow creatures and see farther than the others."

In a book about another animal with mythic importance to humans, it is suggested that the bear "tells us what we were and perhaps what we lost." The giraffe delivered that message to Captain Cornwallis Harris.

> *Loftiest of all the* Mammiferes . . . *the animal before us is one so extraordinary in form, and so stupendous in stature, that even the stuffed spoils, the almost shapeless representative of the living creature produce upon the eye of the beholder a mixed effect of astonishment and awe. Involuntarily is his imagination led back to the early epochs of the world, when colossal beings peopled the earth, and were the undisputed possessors of every region. He fancies himself at once in the presence of one of the survivors of the great diluvian catastrophe, when the Mastodon, the Megatherium, and perhaps its own congeners, were swept away, leaving the camelopardalis [the giraffe's scientific name] to attest, amongst a few others, what were the forms of a primitive animated nature.*
> *—Capt. William Cornwallis Harris, hunter, 1840*

For Frederick Courtenay Selous, the respected British naturalist and hunter whose name now identifies a large animal reserve in Tanzania, giraffes literally opened the doorway to the past.

> *The sight of a herd of giraffes walking leisurely across an open piece of ground, or feeding through a park-like country of scattered trees and bush, is one which, once seen, must ever linger in the memory; for there is something about the appearance of some few of the largest mammals still extant upon the earth which stirs the imagination as the sight of smaller but more beautiful animals can never do. When watching a moose bull standing knee-deep on the edge of some swampy lake, amidst the silence and the gloom of sub-*

*Arctic pine forests, I always seem to be carried back to some far distant period of the world's history; and I remember that when hunting with Bushmen amidst the dull monotony of the sun-scorched, silent wastes of Western South Africa, the sight of giraffes always stirred the same thought. My rude companions were palaeolithic men, and we were hunting strange beasts in the hot dry atmosphere of a long past geological era.*

*—Frederick C. Selous, 1908*

Even when the giraffe became familiar, moving into the science texts and the world's zoos, its impact was stunning.

*To see a giraffe in the cool highlands, with the purple-red African sun setting behind its tall, slim outline, is one of man's great visual experiences. Or to travel through the chill of an African dawn, and see the graceful outline of a herd of giraffes moving across the savanna, gives one a feeling of the world when it was new—when prehistoric beasts populated it.*

*—Bradley Smith, American author, 1972*

I took that trip back in time last summer, when Dr. Nikos Solounias, an evolutionary biologist who is one of the only people now studying fossil giraffes, gave me a private tour of the paleontology cabinets at the American Museum of Natural History in New York. In the cool and musty mélange of bones, skins, teeth, and other skeletal fragments, immense sightless skulls of giraffe ancestors loomed over the countertops. Rock-hard remains of creatures that had shared a slice of prehistory with wooly mammoths and saber-toothed tigers bore the carefully printed labels of dedicated field researchers. One narrow skull, yellowed with fourteen million years of antiquity, bore two sets of slim, pointed horns. Another, a mere two million years old, was crowned with a palmate horn more than a foot wide.

What struck me above all in this zoological vault was that our awe is rooted in size—the powerful, towering height of this most improbable animal. I have stood right next to living giraffes and can vouch that they dwarf even those of us considered tall. But it registered most vividly when Dr. Solounias opened up the museum's storage bins. Reaching into one wide, flat drawer, he pulled out the bleached white femur of a long extinct giraffe ancestor, hardened with the millennia and as thick as my fist. I was amazed by its weight. Then Dr. Solounias moved to another section and dug out the plaster cast of a bone almost two feet long. "It's the metatarsal of a giraffe called *Bohlinia attica*," he told me. "Lived about eight million years ago." He bent down to where my own leg connected to my foot and held his thumb and forefinger a few inches apart. "That's how long ours are."

For a *20/20* story on discrimination against short men, a psychologist told me, "We just assume anybody we're looking up to has power over us. And when you stop and think where that comes from . . . when we were little, and we were all little once, we looked up at our parents." The author of his own book on giraffes recognized that instinct.

*There is no doubt that humans are awed and deeply stirred by anything that is big and this does not apply only to Texans. A monumental building, a big ship or a towering mountain all give us a special thrill, and this may account for the tremendous interest people have always taken in the giraffe. Its tall stature has been stressed in all descriptions, old and new. The elephant is, of course, much more bulky and can attain a weight of 6 tons as against the mere 2800 lb of a big giraffe. The shoulder height of both animals is about the same, but the giraffe carries its head very much higher and can literally look down its nose upon the mightiest elephant.*

*—C. A. W. Guggisberg, 1969*

Curiously, or perhaps not so curiously in a world that invented the "me generation," many of those who succumbed readily to the charms of the giraffe also felt it necessary to question its value. That is, its value to human beings. Of what use is the giraffe? they asked over and over again. The author of one of the earliest credible natural history texts took a hard-nosed approach.

*The giraffe is one of the most beautiful and largest quadrupeds: without being noxious, he is at the same time extremely useless. The enormous disproportion of his legs, of which those before are double the length of those behind, prevents him from exercising his powers. His body has no stability; he has a staggering gait; and his movements are slow and constrained. When at liberty, he cannot escape from his enemies, nor can he serve man in a domestic state.*
—*Buffon, 1781*

A reporter for the *Illustrated London News* of 1926 dismissed the poor creatures after just one visit to the zoo:

*The giraffe is a ruminant—he chews the cud, but he does not ruminate. That is to say, he does not reflect or meditate—he simply chews. He is consumed by nerves, and is full of senseless fears. Wild animals must think or die, but the giraffe owes his survival to his neurotic nerves and exaggerated suspicion. He has no vocal chord, no sense of fun or humour, but is very fond of onions. Apart from his beauty, there is nothing more to be said about the giraffe. . . .*
—Illustrated London News, *1926*

A hunter who wrote novels about Africa exhibited more humility.

*A creature so strangely shaped, and possessing so much speed and strength, was certainly designed by the Creator for some other use than browsing upon the leaves of mimosa trees; but that use, man has not yet discovered.*
—*Capt. Mayne Reid, 1867*

The fact that the giraffe has never been domesticated, and likely never will be, did not concern two modern-day champions of African wildlife.

*Darwin, in the throes and perplexities of giving birth to evolution, confessed that "the sight of a feather in a peacock's tail made me sick whenever I gazed at it." He does not, unfortunately, record what he felt when he looked at a*

*giraffe, except to characterize its tail as an excellent fly dis-
perser. But was there, in cold fact, any simple justification,
any more than there was for the fabulous jewel in the peacock's feather, for that singular creation, that extravagance
of angles, that triangular elongation coated with crazy
paving, the modern and somewhat modest descendant of a
long experiment in giraffedom?*
                                              —Lady Huxley, 1977

*[I]t should not be necessary to consider a giraffe's uses. It is
worthy enough as the world's tallest living creature and as a
graceful if grotesque part of the African scene. . . . Just look
at a giraffe in the wild and see what it is all about. It is a
wonderment of nature—just by being.*
        —Norman Meyers, photographer and writer, 1972

In 1592 a London merchant who happened upon a captive
giraffe in Constantinople, called it "the admirablest and fairest
beast that ever I saw." Two centuries later a pair of French
biologists ticked off its attributes: "Magnificent in appearance,
bizarre in form, unique in gait, colossal in height and inoffensive in character." And recently, a Canadian scientist studying
giraffes in Kenya pointed out that for all its power and
resources, this one-ton skyscraper whose hooves can kick a
death blow almost never harms another being.

    This book seeks to capture all that, and more. I think of it
as a cultural history of giraffes, and I wrote it to explore our
fascination with these fabulous creatures—to examine their
impact on our lives through the ages. And ours on them. I've
also included words and wisdom from the scientists and histo-
rians and explorers who knew them first. As a reporter, I am
well aware that passion alone does not necessarily produce a
good story. On the other hand, it's not a bad place to start.

- They are the tallest quadrupeds, reaching eighteen feet or more for males, a dainty sixteen feet for females. And while the bulls (males) can weigh 1.5 tons, the cows (females) are a trim .5 ton. The record for a giraffe shot by a hunter was a nineteen-foot-three-inch bull from Kenya.

- Their sturdy front legs appear much longer than the rear pair, because their backbone angles down toward the rump. In fact, all four legs are almost the same size, and each lands in a cloven hoof the size of a dinner plate.

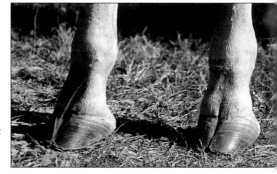

- They are ruminants, which means they chew their cud, and spend most of the hours of each day either devouring the leaves of the acacia tree or reliving the experience.

- One species of the acacia owes its name to the giraffe, and some seeds germinate only after passing through the giraffe's digestive track.

- They come in at least nine different patterns with varying colors, ranging from the traditional brown-on-blond blotches to a rich reddish brown etched with fine white lines. But giraffes themselves make no such distinctions among their peers. Perhaps the most politically correct members of the animal kingdom, they do not discriminate based on the color of other giraffes' skin (mating readily with any other member of the species). They are strict vegetarians and devout pacifists, with neither aggressive nor territorial inclinations.

- Their only natural enemies are the lion and, on occasion, the hyena and the leopard. Humans—who have killed them in the name of sport, or science, or capitalism (the giraffe's tail has been used as a flyswatter, its hide for buckets or shields)—are now forbidden by law to hunt them in the wild.

- Although not endangered, they are often misunderstood and at home subject to human encroachment.

- They are one of the only animals born with horns, which can number up to five and get bonier with age. A short, stiff mane runs the length of their neck.

- Giraffes are not mute. They have vocal cords but rarely use them. They don't need to. Their monumental size lets them see and communicate readily with their eyes.

- They have no tear ducts but have been seen to cry.

- They have never been seen to bathe.

- They sleep only about a half hour a day—usually in the form of five-minute giraffe naps.

- Their amazing necks contain the same number of vertebrae as our own: seven. A special joint enables the giraffe to raise its head vertically in line with the neck and even a bit farther back, a special feature that makes those out-of-the-way leaves easier to nibble.

**Drinking techniques**

• Still, for all its span, the giraffe's neck is too short to reach the ground. As a result, the animal has to spread its legs precariously or kneel down on padded "knees" (which are really wrists) to take a drink.

• Their ability to get that drink—and then jerk their heads up to scout for predators without fainting dead away—is the result of an awesome circulatory system that intrigues NASA as a key to preventing blackouts at high altitudes. It turns out they have an extra large heart and lungs, the highest blood pressure of any mammal, and a marvelous system of blood vessels that prohibits too much flow to the brain when the head is lowered.

• Their gait is just plain weird. For the amble, or slow pace, giraffes move both right legs at once, then both left, a rocking motion that led a Greek writer to say they "always had one side dangling." For the gallop (up to 35 MPH), all four legs seem to leave the ground at once and the neck pumps along rhythmically. An arrangement of muscles like a couch slung on supple springs is the suspension system that lets it glide across the most rugged terrain so smoothly.

• Mating is a brief event, with no apparent emotional attachment, leading to a fifteen-month pregnancy. In the wild, giraffe moms-to-be are modest, seeking privacy to give birth.

They do so standing up. In an hour or so, the baby is born, or rather dropped—nearly six feet tall and often up walking within fifteen minutes.

- Child care can be cooperative, in nurseries formed by groups of cows. Giraffes mature by their fourth year. They can live to almost thirty.

- People who work with them disagree on how smart the giraffe really is, but one expert noted that "an analysis of its brain formation shows the highest development of nervous centre among artiodactyls [cloven-hoofed animals]: the index of its cerebrum is 29.5 compared with 20 in wild cattle and 14 in pigs."

- Although some in Africa still see the giraffe as a source of tasty meat, it is not correct that it was known to Moses and considered kosher. That long held misconception grew out of the misreading of an ancient text.

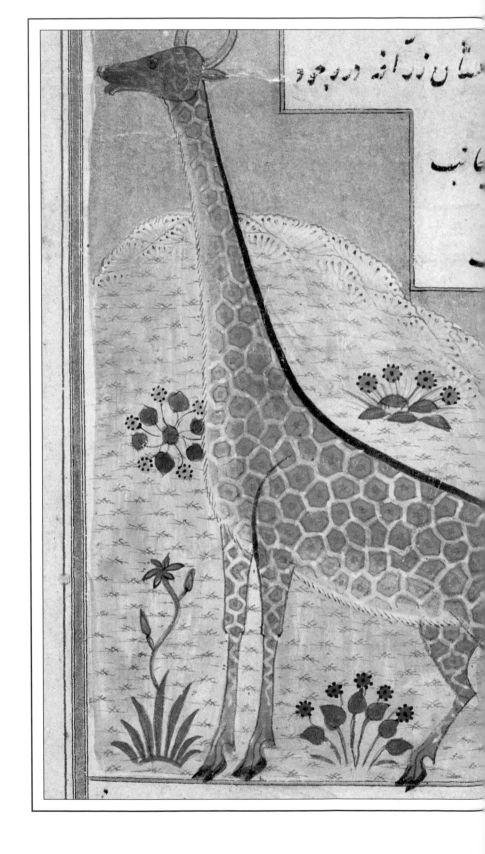

# CHAPTER ONE

# How the Giraffe Got Its Name

**T**HIS CHAPTER might also be called "The Three Blind Men and the Giraffe." Early chroniclers simply did not believe that such an animal could exist. Eyewitnesses were entranced but skeptical; scientists back home receiving their reports—and the first fragments of giraffe skin—were plainly baffled. With its dappled hide, oversize neck, and sloping spine, it just *had* to be something

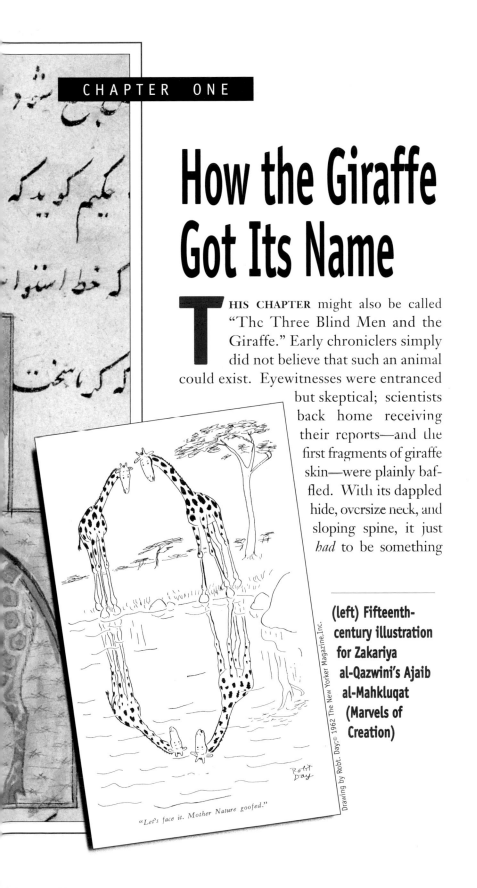

"Let's face it. Mother Nature goofed."

Drawing by Robt. Day.© 1962 The New Yorker Magazine, Inc.

**(left) Fifteenth-century illustration for Zakariya al-Qazwini's Ajaib al-Mahkluqat (Marvels of Creation)**

else—or at least a combination of some things they already understood.

The word "giraffe" comes from the Arabic *zarāfa*, which has been credited with almost as many roots as the giraffe has spots. As a verb it means "to jump" or "to hurry," leading to the noun "one who walks swiftly." It has also been traced to an Ethiopic word that denotes "graceful one." But its primary derivation, in the opinion of a linguistic authority, stems from a source meaning "assemblage," as in assemblage of animals. The Greeks were more specific: they contributed its scientific name, *camelopardalis* (or the more common, *camelopard*), which literally describes a camel's body wearing a leopard's coat. It was the best they could come up with, but it was only the beginning. Ancient texts and imaginative artists stitched together a hybrid barely recognizable as the giraffe we know today. What they lacked in accuracy, they more than made up for in pure creativity. For example:

Illustration from Buffon's
*Histoire Naturelle*, 1801

> *[It has] a neck like a horse, feet and legs like an ox and a head like a camel, and is of a ruddy color picked out with white spots.*
>
> —*Pliny the Elder,*
> Naturalis Historia, *first century* A.D.

> *Tell also, I pray thee, O clear-voiced Muse of diverse tones, of those tribes of wild beasts which are of hybrid nature and mingled of two stocks, even the Pard [leopard] of spotted*

*back joined and united with the Camel. . . . The tender
mouth is sufficiently large, like that of a Stag. . . . The tail
. . . is short, like that of the swift Gazelles. . . .*
                                    —*Oppian, second century* A.D.

Hybrids were apparently all the rage that millennium.
The Greek poet Oppian cited another "double breed," a cross
between the camel and sparrow. We call it an ostrich.

Some years later, in a novel set in the fifth century B.C., a
Greek writer named Heliodorus imagined the confusion that
led to the christening. He described

*a marvelous animal of extraordinary appearance. His size
was about that of a camel; his skin, like that of a leopard,
was decorated with spots in a floral pattern. His hindquar-
ters and belly were low and like a lion's; the shoulders,
forefeet and chest were of a height out of all proportion to
the other members. The neck was slender, and tapered from
the large body to a swanlike throat. The head was shaped
like a camel's and was almost twice as large as that of a
Libyan ostrich. . . . The appearance of this creature astonished
the entire multitude,
and extemporizing a
name for it from the
dominant traits of his
body, they called it
camelopard.*
—*Heliodorus, c.
third century* A.D.

Medieval Arabic
manuscripts offered
readers a wide choice of
genealogies. One poet
wrote that a hyena and
a she-cow would mate
and that the resulting
offspring would couple
with an oryx to produce
a giraffe. Another said

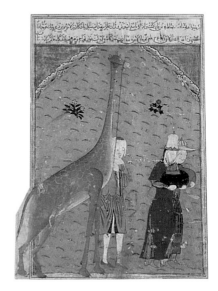

Persian watercolor of the giraffe from
the sultan of Egypt being presented to
Timur, October 1405 (see page 27)

the mongrel nature of the giraffe was explained by the fact "that during summer, beasts and wild animals collect together in the watering places, and have promiscuous sexual intercourse with one another . . . sometimes several males mount the same animal, thus causing the seminal fluids to be mixed up; and in consequence of it, the females give birth to animals varying in appearance, colours, and forms." For instance:

> *The giraffe lives in Nubia. It is said that it takes its place between the panther and the camel mare, that the panther mates with the latter who produces the giraffe.*
> —*Abu Bakr Ibn al-faqih, Arabic geographer c. 1022*

> *The giraffe is produced by the camel mare, the male hyena, and the wild cow. Its head is shaped like that of a stag, its horns like that of cattle, its legs like those of a nine-year-old camel, its hoof like those of cattle, its tail like that of a gazelle; its neck is very long, its hands are long, and its feet are short.*
> —*Zakariya al-Qazwini,*
> *author of a Persian bestiary, 1203–83*

> *The Persians call it* ushtur gâw palank, *because* ushtur *is a camel,* gâw *a cow, and* palank *a hyena.*
> —*Damiri, author of an animal anthology, 1371*

As early as the tenth century, Damiri had correctly reported that the giraffe was a species unto itself, since it can reproduce itself. But few heard or listened. They weren't even certain of its coloring. Albert the Great, the German scholar who would later be canonized as Saint Albertus Magnus, wrote a natural history in which he mentioned the giraffe's "reddish color speckled with white spots." Two Venetian travelers to Persia saw it as "a violet color mingled all over with black spots." Little wonder this Florentine voyager to Cairo gave up:

> *The Giraffe is almost like the ostrich, save that its chest has no feathers but has a very white fine wool, and a horse's tail . . . it has horse's feet and bird's legs . . . and the head is like a horse's, and is white, and it has two horns like a wether [male sheep], and it eats barley and bread like a horse. And*

# What's in a Name?

The Egyptian hieroglyph for giraffe means "to prophesy, "to foretell," which has been taken as evidence of its keen eyesight.

Ancient Arabic words include *saraphah*, *gyrapha*, *gyraffa*, and *zirafa*. The Persians also called it *ushturgao* ("camel-cow"). To the Chaldeans it was *deba*, and *ana*, which may be related to *nabun*, used by Pliny.

The encyclopedist Vincent de Beauvais, in his *Speculum Naturale* (1225), described it under three different names (*anabulla*, *camelopardo*, and *orasius*), apparently without realizing it. Albertus Magnus repeated the mistake in his thirteenth-century *De Animalibus*, using *anabula*, *camelopardulus*, and *oraflus*.

*Anabula* probably comes from the Ethiopians, who called it *nabin*; and *orafle* was used in Old French. In modern French it's *girafe*, in Italian *giraffa*, in German *giraffe*, in Afrikaans *kameelperd* and in Zulu *indlulamethi*. But my personal favorite is the Swahili word— *twiga*—which just sounds the way a giraffe looks.

*the Sultan has four of these animals. It really is a very deformed thing to see.*
*—Simone Sigoli, Florentine traveler, 1384*

The general bewilderment—matched inaccuracy for inaccuracy by some equally unscientific paintings, woodcuts, and engravings—results from the remote geography and history of this exotic creature. Many of those who wrote about giraffes, and most of the people who drew pictures of them centuries ago, had never seen one. And many who did got it wrong anyway. A French professor who looked long and closely enough to sketch a giraffe in 1826, admitted that after considerable attention he could not recall its shape and held "only an uncertain memory of its carriage." That, he said, is why one needs to see it often, since each new look "occasions several new observations."

Its shape *was* baffling, confounding virtually everyone who tried to understand it. A correspondent for the *London Spectator* gazed at a newcomer to the zoo in 1895 and noted "the strangeness of its proportions":

> *Yet it is not strange that the first accounts of the giraffe were discredited by some who pronounced it an "impossible animal," not on the ground on which some botanists pronounced the old pictures of the "cyclamen narcissus" to be those of an "impossible flower," because it appeared to be a compound of two incompatible types, but from the anatomical difficulties suggested by the drawings.*
>
> —Spectator, *1895*

**Buffon, 1781**

Well, what would you draw if someone described it as tall, with a long neck, a spine that pitched downward and spots all over its body?

These irresistible but inept images illustrate the tenuous understanding of those who were not used to seeing giraffes. People who lived with them got it right.

The first known humans to encounter giraffes lived five thousand years ago and were so taken with their long-limbed neighbors, they painted and carved them on their caves. Superb prehistoric frescoes—some of naturalistically rendered giraffes more than twenty-five feet high—have been found on a sandstone plateau called Tassili n'Ajjer in the

Sahara desert in southern Algeria. This magnificent record of a climate and era long gone recalls a time when the desert truly bloomed; when, in the words of the archaeologist who discovered many of the paintings, the land was marked by "the grassy vales, the forest glades, the pools and all the beasts of what must have been an earthly paradise."

The Sahara is believed to have started drying up about five thousand years ago, but giraffes apparently lingered for some time after that. Rock and cave artists across North Africa have left vivid evidence of giraffes' prominence in their lives. They etched giraffe pictures onto perpendicular stones and outlined their shapes on flat outcroppings. One

Top right: Author at Silozwane Cave, Zimbabwe; middle left: chiseled giraffes and "plate nets" used to capture them, Fezzan, Sahara; bottom right: chiseled giraffe with painted design and two humans, Fezzan, Sahara; bottom left, middle right: rock carvings from Namibia

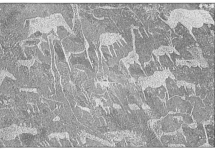

stunning set of larger-than-life engravings at Fezzan, in present-
day Libya, details giraffes being trapped, captured, and perhaps
simply admired, some with intricate lines outlining their manes
and the pattern on their hide.

The images extend to southern Africa, as well, where they
are attributed to Stone Age ancestors of the Bushmen, or San
people. Many of the finest paintings adorn the walls of the caves
in Zimbabwe's stunning Matopos Hills, a breathtakingly beautiful terrain of immense granite boulders and endless vistas south
of Bulawayo. On a recent trip there I eagerly climbed the steep
precipices leading to two of the best preserved caves: Nswatugi
and Silozwane. At Nswatugi, I was rewarded by a pair of giraffes,
the larger about two feet tall, painted in red ochre untold thousands of years ago. A running giraffe, at least three feet high, was
drawn off to the side. At Silozwane, some 200 yards up a cliff that
felt perpendicular, I marveled at three more splendid creations,
each higher than my reach.

The drawings in these prehistoric art galleries continue to fas-
cinate and mystify modern researchers, many of whom now
believe they carry magic or spiritual or religious significance.
"[T]he art is unlikely to have been simply decorative or narrative,
painting for pleasure . . ." writes archaeologist Nick Walker. It is
"rich in symbolism and contributed in some powerful way to the
smooth functioning of the community." He points out that
among the many animal species respresented—including humans,
antelopes, insects, and birds—"giraffe are often large, elaborate,
and central paintings in big living sites . . . and perhaps represent
senior shamans or headmen. . . . The correlation of giraffe with
large camps and their dominant position on panels also encour-
ages the idea that they were connected with group well-being or
social relationships."

**Contemporary hut, Zimbabwe**

The durability of this
tradition is impressive. In
1904 a visitor to an Acholi
village in Uganda described
their bamboo houses with
interior walls of smoothed
black mud. All bore painted
designs in red, white, or pale
gray. "The giraffe appears

very often," he noticed, "and not infrequently the figure of a man is placed just above the giraffe's head. This indicates that the owner of the hut has killed a giraffe."

I found similar images on huts in a village in Zimbabwe. Just for the record, giraffes decorate my walls, too. Only I didn't have to kill any.

**Ancient Egyptian palette with two giraffes**

Giraffes were also popular in Egypt's Nile Valley civilization, not as wild animals but as prized captives. One of the earliest renderings (perhaps 3400 B.C.), on a slate palette used for grinding eye makeup, shows two stylized giraffes in profile. Giraffes also turn up on pre-dynastic Egyptian ivories, gold axhandles, and pottery.

The first known expedition in search of a giraffe was authorized by Queen Hatshepsut, around 1500 B.C. No doubt aware that giraffes, like all wild animals, greatly enhanced a leader's power, she dispatched her fleet down the Red Sea to Somalia, then known as the Land of Punt. Five boatloads of treasures returned: perfumes, ivory, monkeys,

Painted cast copy of a wall in the temple of Beit el-Wali, built in Nubia by Rameses II. The giraffe being presented by the Nubians to the pharaoh is joined by a leopard and monkeys.

greyhounds, African birds, and a giraffe, whose image remains on her tomb in Thebes.

A giraffe decorated the temple tombs of a number of other Egyptian rulers, too, a testimony to its respected position in their kingdoms. Tutankhamen, the boy-king, was given two when he defeated the Nubians. Rameses II reportedly had several.

By the time the Greeks conquered Egypt and took over the pharaohs' jobs, giraffes had become the tribute animal of choice, a mighty show of strength over a vanquished foe. Ptolemy II included a live giraffe in his triumphal pageant at Alexandria after defeating the armies of Antiochus I. The parade, a mile-long menagerie that would have done Cecil B. DeMille proud, led off with twenty-four chariots drawn by 96 elephants, each wearing a gold garland. There were 8 pairs of ostriches in harness, 2,400 hounds, more than 300 sheep, 24 lions, 16 cheetahs, 14 leopards, 14 oryx, 12 camels, cages full of brilliantly colored birds, a python, a black rhinoceros, and a lone giraffe, among other animals. The entire assemblage, convened for the Feast of Dionysus, has been called "the world's most magnificent orgy."

But while kings paraded them and cavemen painted them, no one wrote about giraffes until about 104 B.C. That distinction goes not to Aristotle, who makes no mention of them, but to another Greek scholar, Agatharchides. He foreshadowed centuries of amazed commentary by remarking on their portmanteau name, their great size, and their long necks. Strabo, the Greek geographer, later added his surprise at a physical trait that would startle virtually everyone who saw giraffes: their sloped backs. "Their hinder parts are so much lower than their front parts that they appear to be seated on their tail parts," said Strabo. He noted that it was clearly "a domesticated animal, for it shows no sign of a savage disposition."

Pliny the Elder expressed some disappointment over that docility in the giraffe Julius Caesar brought to Rome in 46 B.C. It was the first in Europe since prehistory, but it apparently did not live up to the advance billing. In his *Natural History*, Pliny wrote that it was "more remarkable for appearance than for ferocity."

Caesar didn't mind.  Setting off a cruel custom that would symbolize the worst of the Roman Empire, he consecrated his newly built Forum by sacrificing the giraffe and four hundred lions in a bloody spectacle open to the public.  The carnage was just beginning.

A subsequent emperor, Commodus, took an even more sadistic interest in the slaughter of wild animals at these so-called circus games.  He personally went into the public arena and killed elephants, hippopotamuses, rhinoceroses, tigers, one hundred bears (the latter in a single day), and at least one giraffe.  Earlier, the poet Horace had chided his fellow citizens for relishing the "circus," citing the Greek philosopher and early moralist Democritus:

> *Democritus, if he were still on earth,*
> *would deride a throng gazing with open*
> *mouth at a beast half camel, half panther,*
> *or at a white elephant.*
> > —*Horace, after* 17 B.C.

**Roman sarcophagus, second century A.D., complete with elegant spotted giraffe**

More civilized Romans preferred their giraffes in more civilized settings: mosaics, frescoes, and meticulously detailed coffins. A well-preserved sarcophagus from the late second century A.D. depicts the same Dionysian celebration Ptolmey re-created in Alexandria, this time carved in stone, with a fine representation of a giraffe. This was clearly a popular theme, as another carving of the same drunken festivities to the god of wine, complete with satyrs, elephants, and giraffe, surrounds a third-century Roman sarcophagus. And in 1996 the stunning mosaic floor of a third-century Roman villa was uncovered in Israel. Among the wildlife traced in tiny squares of stone: one very jaunty giraffe.

Starting around the fifth century, a long line of giraffes was given to the rulers of Constantinople. The one presented to the Byzantine emperor in 1257 was promenaded in the streets for several days to amuse the citizens, then sheltered in the menagerie at the palace. The Ottoman rulers of Turkey maintained the tradition, and a sixteenth-century eyewitness wrote that the "Great Turk"—Sultan Mohammed II—customarily marched to war accompanied by a parade of men and beasts. The dogs wore gold, velvet, and scarlet cloth; the tame lions and elephants walked peacefully; and the giraffe, "beinge prince of all the beasts, was ledd by three chaines of three sondry men stalkinge before him."

The rest of Europe was reintroduced to giraffes in 1215, when the sultan of Egypt gave one to Frederick II, king of Naples and the Two Sicilies and later Germany. Frederick, whose interest in natural science was well-known, added the "odd strutting" creature to his collection of lions, lynxes, leopard, camels, eunuchs, and Saracen girls and gave the sultan a white bear in return. Albertus Magnus noted in *De Animalibus* that he had seen Frederick's giraffe, a rare opportunity that does not account for his describing it under three different names.

During the 1400s, the rulers of Italy engaged in a spirited rivalry of private animal collections. Owning a giraffe gave one a considerable advantage, which may be why the dukes of Naples and Calabria enjoyed such enviable status. In 1459 Cosimo de' Medici showed off his giraffe to Pope Pius II in Florence and tried to replicate the circus of his forebears by putting the poor creature in the public square with a wild boar, four bulls, two horses, and two lions. The event failed miserably. In one account, the lions—exhausted from their march through the streets—refused to attack and lay down while the terrified giraffe huddled against a fence. Several decades later, Lorenzo, the greatest Medici of all, would display his giraffe with far more humane, and successful, consequences (see chapter 7).

In Asia, the arrival of the animal from Africa took on geopolitical significance. In 1404 the sultan of Egypt sent a giraffe to Timur, better known as Tamerlane the Great, whose celebrated conquests of Oriental lands made him a ruler well worth courting. A Spaniard named Ruy Gonzalez de Clavijo, the envoy of King Henry II, met up with the spotted traveler in Azerbaijan and was thunderstruck by the accompanying caravan of twenty horses, fifteen camels, and six ostriches. Gonzalez de Clavijo called the strange new creature *jornufa*:

> *The length of the foreleg from the shoulder down to the hoof measured, in this present beast sixteen palms, and from the breast thence up to the top of the head measured likewise sixteen palms: and when the beast raised its head it was a wonder to see the length of the neck. . . . The hind legs in comparison with the forelegs were short, so that any one seeing the animal casually and for the first time would imagine it to be seated and not standing. . . . The belly is white but the rest of the body is of yellow golden hue cross marked with broad white bands. . . . The animal reaches so high when it extends its neck that it can overtop any wall, even one with six or seven coping stones in the height, and when it wishes to eat it can stretch up to the branches of any high tree, and only of green leaves is its food. To one who never saw the Giraffe before this beast is indeed a very wonderous sight to behold.*
> *—Ruy Gonzalez de Clavijo, early 1400s*

Tamerlane's giraffe, sent to celebrate his grandchild's wedding, proved a hardy voyager. By the time it was officially presented at the court in Samarkand, along with all the ambassadors of Asia, it had walked the entire way from Cairo, a distance of more than three thousand miles.

**The Reuwich giraffe, 1486**

The first giraffe in China had a more relaxed voyage, sailing by ship from India in 1414. But its reception was unparalleled and its influence vast, as you will learn in chapter 8.

As travel became more accessible during the Middle Ages and beyond, it was the people who went to the giraffe—always, the captive giraffe. The first Englishman to describe one was Sir Thomas Mandeville (or Maundeville), who claimed to be an English knight on the road from 1322 to 1356. More likely "Mandeville" was the nom de plume of a talented plagiarist. One critic said, "Mandeville's longest journey was to the nearest library." Still, his book was widely read in Europe and was known to have been consulted by such notables as Leonardo da Vinci and Christopher Columbus. So his description would have carried great influence:

> *In Arabye is a kind of beast that some men call Garsantes, that is a fayre beast, and he is hyer than a great courser or a stead, but his neck is nere XX cubytes long, and his crop and his taile lyke a hart and he may loke over a high house.*

The first image in print was done by Erhard Reuwich for a book published in 1486. *Peregrinationes in Terram Sanctam* is an account of a pilgrimage in the Holy Land, during which the German author Bernhard von Breydenbach claims to have seen a giraffe at the palace in Cairo. Unfortunately the woodcut looks exactly like an antelope, and its frequent repetition in later publications added little to public knowledge. Bernhard Laufer, a curator at Chicago's Field Museum of Natural History, who compiled much of this information for his 1928 brochure, *The Giraffe in History and Art*, commented dryly, "I am inclined to presume that Reuwich drew the picture of the giraffe from memory and that in his effort to remember it visions of the oryx may have crossed his mind; at any rate, some mishap has occurred to him."

PORTRAICT DE LA GIRAFFE

Though stiff and inaccurate, these early distorted giraffe images, usually more charming than correct, nonetheless became part of the growing emphasis on science and the emergence of the

(left)Pierre Belon's giraffe, 1553; (below) André Thevet gave the giraffe short hind legs and callous captors.

scientifically based natural history. In the middle of the sixteenth century, two French naturalists, Pierre Gilles d'Albi and André Thevet, traveled to Egypt, where they saw giraffes in the castle in Cairo. Thevet published his observations in two subsequent books, in which he pointed out the length of the giraffe's neck (longer than a camel's) and the three horns on its head. He did, however, repeat the centuries-old blunder about the hind legs being shorter than the front legs. Thevet also provided two woodcuts of the beast, one of which he insisted was "as near natural as possible." The apology did not improve his precision, but it was a step in the right direction.

At about the same time, a French voyager named Pierre Belon, saw the same giraffes in Cairo and published his version of reality in 1553. He got the giraffe's placid disposition perfectly— "une beste moult belle et de la plus doulce nature qui soit"—but gave its neck too many curves and its body too many lumps.

Ironically, the most important European naturalists of this period, whose texts informed generations of scholars, never laid eyes on a living giraffe. Konrad Gesner, a Swiss physician, published the first volume of his *Historia Animalium* (in Latin) in 1551. That became the basis for Edward Topsell's *The Historie of Four-footed Beasts*, in 1607, the first such English-language bestiary, combining both fact and fiction from his predecessors:

> *The head thereof is like to a Camels, the neck to a Horses, the body to a Harts; and his cloven hoof is the same with a Camels: the colour of this Beast is for the most part red and white, mixed together, therefore very beautifull to behold, by relation of the variable and interchangeable skin, being full of spots: but yet they are not always of one colour. He hath two little horns growing on his head of the colour of iron, his eyes rowling and frowing, his mouth but small like a Harts, his tongue is neer three foot long, and with that he will so speedily gather in his meat, that the eyes of man will fail to behold his hast, and his neck diversly coloured, is fifteen feet long, which he holdesth up higher than a Camels, and far above the proportion of his other parts. His forefeet are much longer then his hinder and therefore his back declineth towards his buttocks, which are very like an Asses. The pace of this beast differeth*

*from all other in the world, for he doth not move his right and left foot one after another, but both together, and so likewise the other, whereby his whole body is removed at every step or strain.*

—*Edward Topsell*

Topsell, an English curate, covered himself by noting that the camelopard's spots (most likely he was describing a reticulated giraffe) were "wrought in fashion of a fishers net, and the whole body so admirably intercoloured with variety, that is it in vain for the wit or art of man, once to go about to endevour the emulous

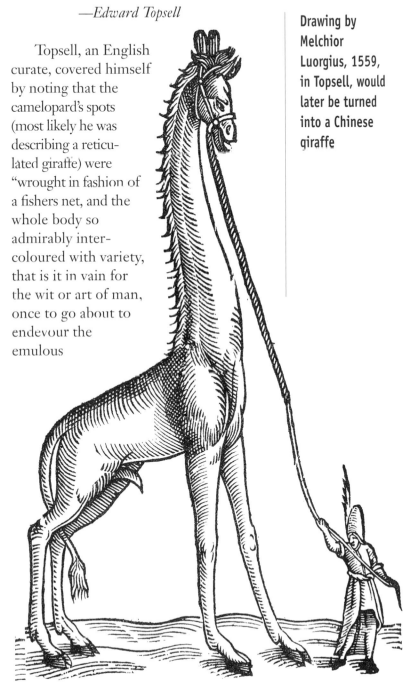

Drawing by Melchior Luorgius, 1559, in Topsell, would later be turned into a Chinese giraffe

imitation thereof." Then he included two very different images: the Reuwich antelope-as-giraffe, next to a more evocative woodcut by another artist. The latter lacks spots and exaggerates the neck but at least captures its spirit. In an amusing plagiarism of the most flattering sort, the drawing was copied by a Jesuit missionary for a volume he had published in China. In that version the keeper and backdrop had metamorphosed into Chinese. The same image also looks hauntingly similar to the one in the zoological work of Bolognese professor Ulisse Aldrovandi, published after his death in 1622.

When a real artist got a good look, the results were significantly better. The Renaissance artist Gentile Bellini spent four years in Constantinople as court painter to Sultan Mohammed II, where he saw the giraffes in the sultan's famed menagerie. When Bellini returned home to Venice, he placed one of the gentle creatures in his famed *Preaching of St. Mark at Alexandria*. Unfinished at his death in 1507, it was completed by his brother, Giovanni. The graceful animal looks very much like a giraffe.

But for all the charming illustrations, for all the descriptions, the giraffe still eluded widespread public understanding. By 1613 an English traveler expanded its dubious lineage by claiming it was created by crossing a leopard, a hart, a buffalo, and a camel. A Scotsman named Fynes Morison, who traveled to Constantinople in 1597, found the giraffe in the palace menagerie (then sharing its compartment in the old Palace of Constantine with an elephant) both awesome and a bit unsettling. Aware of the widespread ignorance, he carefully related his meeting in 1617 with

> *another beast newly brought out of Affricke, (the Mother of Monsters) which beast is altogether unknowne in our parts . . . and because the beast is very rare, I will describe his forme as well as I can. His haire is red coloured, with many blacke and white spots; I could scarce reach with the points of my fingers to the hinder part of his backe, which grew higher and higher towards his foreshoulder, and his necke was thinne and some three els long, so as hee easily*

*turned his head in a moment to any part or corner of the
roome wherein he stood, putting it over the beames therof,
being built like a Barne, and high (for the Turkish building . . .) by reason whereof he many times put his nose in
my necke, when I thought myselfe furthest distant from
him, which familiarity of his I liked not; and howsoever
the Keepers assured me he would not hurt me, yet I avoided
these his familiar kisses as much as I could.*
                           —*Fynes Morison,* Itinerary, *1617*

Morison's guide tipped the giraffe's keeper for the experience.

These pioneering globe-trotters and scientists did manage
to convey the essence of the animal, but it was not until the
middle of the eighteenth century, when the giraffe was
observed in its native habitat, that anything approaching zoological accuracy was approached. More than four hundred
years earlier, Marco Polo wrote that he had seen giraffes in
Africa, but he neglected to provide any new details. Nicolo de
Conti, who traveled with him and wrote his own account, adds
only that women would interweave giraffe tail hairs with precious stones and wear them from their arms. This sort of activity would later have grim consequences (see Chapter 6) but
contributed little to science.

Leo Africanus, an Arab who converted to Christianity,
wrote a book somewhat later that explained why he did so little to enlighten:

*This beast is so savage and wilde, that it is a very rare mat-
ter to see any of them: for they hide themselves among the
deserts and woodes, where no other beasts use to come; and
so soone as one of them espieth a man, it flieth foorthwith,
though not very swiftly.*
                           —*Leo Africanus, 1526*

So in 1761, when a group of South African settlers and soldiers captured a baby giraffe in the area called Namaqualand
(just south of present-day Namibia), it was quite as revolution-
ary for science as the political upheaval taking place across the
seas in the American colonies. Keep in mind, Africa was a
three-month sail, at best, from England. Europeans hadn't a

clue about the African interior. And when anyone thought about giraffes, if they believed they existed at all, it was assumed they came only from northern parts of the continent—Ethiopia and Sudan in particular. White settlers had been at the Cape since the seventeenth century and had seen giraffes there, but their accounts went unnoticed. Now one was in custody—the first giraffe caught in the wild by Westerners—and despite a predictably self-centered perspective (that the shape of its body and peculiar gait made it "unthinkable that this animal can be employed for any useful purpose"), the colonists performed a major favor to the scientific community. When the calf died, they sent its skin, along with a sketch, to a professor in Holland. He in turn produced a drawing that earned its place in the record books as the first printed image of a wild giraffe.

It appeared in a 1770 edition of Buffon's *Histoire Naturelle*, an important work that helped pave the way for a scientific understanding of the natural world. The author's full name was Georges-Louis Leclerc, comte de Buffon, a professor of natural history in Paris. He published what would become a thirty-six-volume series with numerous editions, some printed posthumously, each filled with the very latest information about the animals or plants or minerals of the world.

One of the more engaging aspects of Buffon's work is the use of different images of giraffes in various editions. He tapped every available source to keep his readers *au courant*. For example, when the British naval captain Philip Carteret drew a giraffe from life in South Africa in 1769, he understood that he was looking at a "scarce and curious animal" and sent his drawing of the animal he called *Camelopardalis* to the Zoological Society in London. "As the existence of this fine animal has been doubted by many," he wrote, "if you think it may offer any pleasure to the curious, you will make what use of it you please."

Buffon copied Carteret's drawing for a new edition of the *Histoire Naturelle*. Its archaic pose and outlandish size may seem familiar, because it has become the very symbol of the genre, copied frequently to this day on decorative items.

Now the flow of knowledge advanced rapidly. A Dutch zoologist wrote the first scientific paper on the giraffe in 1786, based on some skins, a skeleton, and a paper written by a countryman who had dissected the first in South Africa. The

French naturalist François LeVaillant saw his first giraffe there in 1783 and published an enthusiastic account thirteen years later. Few believed that this fantastic spotted animal existed, but they had to take him seriously when he sent a giraffe skin to Paris. Unfortunately the sorry state of the skin, and of taxidermy itself, forced museum officials to patch it with a calfskin. Since no one knew how to stuff it, the beast so graceful in nature wound up with its neck sticking straight up, thus resembling, in one historian's opinion, a swan on the defensive.

Mounting a beast that had not been seen in action led to a number of unsuccessful models. A British wildlife enthusiast pronounced one at the Cape Town Museum a "misshapen monstrosity" and said the specimen in the London Museum was "wretchedly set up, and gives no sort of idea of the animal in its natural state."

**Buffon's copy of the Carteret giraffe, a contemporary classic**

It would take another half century to get the details straight, but now there was no turning back. With interest in, and knowledge about, giraffes soaring, animal providers around the world moved to capitalize on the trend. In 1805 a dealer named George Wombwell brought the first live giraffes to England. From 1826 to 1828, live giraffes arrived in Paris, London, and Vienna, each a gift from the pasha of Egypt to the reigning monarch (see chapter 7). The animal sent to Vienna was welcomed with a grand formal ball and a newly invented dance best translated as the giraffe trot.

America saw its first giraffes a decade later, courtesy of some enterprising capitalists who captured and transported a pair from the Kalahari desert of South Africa. Some evidence indicates that they arrived in Boston in 1837, but conflicting— perhaps overzealous—documents put their U.S. debut in New York in 1838, at a pavilion on lower Broadway, attracting hundreds of paying spectators daily. Then the female was taken to Philadelphia, where, for two weeks in October "and positively no longer," according to the advertisement, she was exhibited on Chesnut (that's how they spelled it) Street, below Tenth, along with an ibex, an eland, and a bontebok (antelope) for the admission price of twenty-five cents—half as much for children under ten. The promoters called her a "stupendous, majestic, and beautiful animal . . . not only the tallest of all known creatures, but the rarest and most singular character." After pointing out that the expedition to catch the giraffes had cost more than $30,000, they cloaked their pitch in flattery: "The intelligence and national pride of the American people will doubtless appreciate and remunerate the adventurous undertaking."

Americans gladly paid for the privilege of viewing this legendary creature and would continue to require giraffes in their zoos (see chapter 9). But the regular appearance of real live animals neither quelled the excitement nor lessened the hype. Giraffes became a featured staple of traveling circuses, with Barnum & Bailey displaying a herd of ten by the 1880s. When the giraffes in the big top died out, leaving only one by the end of the century, the Ringling Bros. publicity machine tantalized would-be circus-goers with a headline as phony as the old fable about the camel and the leopard:

Ringling Bros. ad, 1901

# THE FAR SIDE

By GARY

Giraffe evolution

# CHAPTER TWO

# How the Giraffe Got Its Neck

Cartoonist Gary Larson may have gotten it right. Some early members of the giraffe family *did* have short necks and long legs, although what precisely they looked like in those ancient epochs before humans or cameras remains at best an educated guess. The relatively few fossilized bones that have been discovered don't reveal skin color or spots or even exact shape. Nor, of course, do they explain the transition into the animal we know today. We can confirm that they grew their lovely long necks by elongating their seven vertebral bones—the same number we (and nearly all mammals) have—not by adding more. For what reason? No one knows. But there are intriguing possibilities.

Paleontologists agree that very distant giraffe ancestors were in Africa at least seventeen million years ago. But around the middle of the Miocene epoch, some of them wandered off to Europe and Asia, easily traversing the bridges of land then connecting the continents. About thirty-five extinct species have been identified. Among them: *Sivatherium*, a short-necked animal the size of a small elephant, with a massive rack of horns, that roamed India and Africa; *Giraffokeryx*, the size and shape of an elk, with a slightly longer neck and four pointed horns; *Samotherium*, with an even longer neck, a face like a deer, a body as big as a moose, and two sharp, pointed horns. Its bones were found on the Greek island of Samos.

The sparse fossil record makes the line of descent fuzzy, but the most likely ancestor of the beast we know was an elk-sized creature named *Palaeotragus* that was found near Athens. It is linked to the present by one of its presumed descendants also found near Athens: the long-necked, long-legged *Bohlinia attica*, whose bones are the ones I saw in those museum drawers in New York. The most likely scenario is that about five million years ago, as the climate in Asia and Europe grew cooler and dryer, animals that had evolved from *Palaeotragus* and *Bohlinia* (or perhaps from a common ancestor) ambled back to Africa. Thus, modern giraffes may well be immigrants to the continent we now see as their homeland.

Their long necks were by then well established, but not the secret of their origin. And while popular science has made giraffes the very symbol of the evolutionary process, the real story is more complicated. Almost any text you read maintains that in 1809 Jean Baptiste Pierre Antoine de Monet, better known as Lamarck, the French naturalist, wrote that by stretching for higher and higher foliage, the giraffe elongated its neck, then passed it on to the next generation. Fifty years later, the story continues, Charles Darwin discredited Lamarck's theory by writing that genetic variations occur randomly, accidentally, and that evolution takes place by the natural selection of the individuals best adapted to the current environment. Although he wasn't acknowledged until later, Gregor Mendel made it clear that all the stretching in the world couldn't be passed on in the genes. In other words, the giraffe's long neck was not a matter of will; it was a mistake or mutation that worked. Giraffes with longer necks survived; everyone else didn't.

As it turns out, while the principle is valid, there is less than meets the eye to this legendary clash of the scientists.

Historian of science Richard Burkhardt points out that Lamarck's reference to the giraffe was his sole paragraph on the animal, based on absolutely no data, and was thus not of great significance to him. In fact, Lamarck was more concerned with the capacity of living beings to change and adapt. "Today, however, the major features of Lamarck's biological theorizing have been fogotten while the giraffe example remains to caricature Lamarck's thinking."

# Credibility

Who could believe an ant in theory?
a giraffe in blueprint?
Ten thousand doctors of what's possible
could reason half the jungle out of being.
—John Ciardi, 1984


In an exhaustive essay on the subject in *Natural History* magazine, evolutionary biologist and zoology professor Stephen Jay Gould demonstrates that Darwin never even mentioned the giraffe's neck as an evolutionary example in his first edition of *The Origin of Species* in 1859. In 1868 he conjectured that the neck lengthened gradually, so that the supporting framework of muscle and bone would be in place. But only in his 1872 edition did Darwin address the issue of the neck and natural selection—and then only to refute a critic.

So if Lamarck and Darwin did not really disagree, and if neither shed much light on the subject, whence the long neck? It is tempting to look up in the trees and conclude that the competition for food made a long neck essential; that growing such a neck gave giraffes the ability to outreach antelopes and unevolved giraffes who were stuck closer to the ground. But that, according to Gould, is merely "a perfectly plausible idea for which there is zero evidence. If it's really so good to eat top leaves," he asked me rhetorically, "why giraffes and nothing else?" In his monthly *Natural History* column Gould added, "Giraffes provide no established evidence whatsoever for the mode of evolution of their undeniably useful necks. . . .

We cannot know the reasons for historical origin by listing current uses."

Dr. Nikos Solounias, who also teaches anatomy at the New York College of Osteopathic Medicine, believes it is just as likely that their necks evolved for mating purposes—so that males could perform their ritual dominance battles and preserve the species (see chapter 4). Others have suggested that the legs evolved first, to run from carnivores; then the neck grew to stretch down for water. The point is, the giraffe neck is so useful, it could have solved any number of problems. All we know for sure is that giraffes have been basically unchanged for about two million years, that there is only one species alive today, and that they possess, in Darwin's words, an "admirably coordinated structure."

The giraffe is the only living member of its genus (*Giraffa*) but joins the other even-toed ungulates, or hoofed mammals, in the order Artiodactyla, which has been described as "an order about as exclusive as the telephone book." Alphabetically, the list runs from antelopes to yaks, meaning giraffes share some of their roots with deer, pigs, and even sheep. But that was then. Today a giraffe family reunion (family: Giraffidae) would include just one close living relative—the okapi, a shy, horse-sized, velvet-skinned resident of the deep rain forests of central Africa. Horizontal lines marking its legs and rump give the okapi its distinctive look. It is called a "living fossil," or "primitive survivor," because it is believed to have survived basically unchanged for fifteen million years in the isolated cover of its primitive environment. When the existence of the okapi was confirmed in the Belgian Congo (now Congo) in 1901, it created an immense sensation, "the last and only large mammal to escape the notice of science until the twentieth century," according to a one paleontologist. Today the mysterious beast that was once known only to pygmy hunters can be visited at nearly two dozen zoos in the United States and Europe, where the okapi will literally take you back to the future. Scientists say this zebra-striped, short-necked cousin probably looks more like a primitive giraffe than anything else on earth.

Zebra stripes on a giraffe? Remember, we don't know what designs they wore back then. Skins don't fossilize. But scientists have made up for lost time by thoroughly scrutinizing and categorizing the brilliant tapestries that now adorn giraffes. Their spots are used to sort them out, and while the conclusions are not entirely objective, and there is substantial overlap in the groups, it is generally agreed that there are at least nine subspecies, or varieties.

The most distinctive, once designated as its own species, is the reticulated giraffe (*Giraffa camelopardalis reticulata*), with large, polygonal, liver-colored spots outlined by a network of bright white lines. The

Okapi

smooth-edged blocks may sometimes appear deep red and may also cover the legs. I'm probably biased, because these were the first giraffes I ever saw in the wild, but I think the "retics" are the stars of the species. They are also the most populous zoo giraffe. Range: northeastern Kenya, Ethiopia, Somalia.

The variety you are most likely to encounter in East Africa is the Masai giraffe (*Giraffa camelopardalis tippelskirchi*), with jagged-edged, vine-leaf-shaped spots of dark chocolate on a yellowish background. The spots go all the way down the lower legs. Range: central and southern Kenya, Tanzania.

Thanks to conservation efforts, you can now see more of the Baringo, or Rothschild, giraffe (*Giraffa camelopardalis rothschildi*), named for Lord Lionel Walter Rothschild, a respected zoologist. The spots are deep brown, blotched or rectangular, with poorly defined cream lines. Hocks may also be spotted. Range: Uganda, north-central Kenya (see chapter 7).

The Nubian, or northern, giraffe (*Giraffa camelopardalis camelopardalis*) has large, four-sided spots of chestnut brown

**Reticulated giraffe**

on an off-white background and no spots on inner sides of the legs or below the hocks. Range: eastern Sudan, northeast Congo. Scarcer and much rarer is the Kordofan giraffe (*Giraffa camelopardalis antiquorum*), with smaller, more irregular spots that do cover the inner legs. Range: western and southwestern Sudan. Equally rare is the Nigerian giraffe (*Giraffa camelopardalis peralta*), whose numerous pale, yellowish red spots are now visible only in Chad. It is extinct in Nigeria.

Southern Africa is home to three varieties. The most common is the Cape giraffe (*Giraffa camelopardalis giraffa*, or *capensis*), with rounded or blotched spots, some with starlike extensions on a light tan ground, running down to the hooves. Range: South Africa, Namibia, Botswana, Zimbabwe, Mozambique.

Angola and Zambia give us the Angola giraffe (*Giraffa camelopardalis angolensis*), with large spots and some notches

**Masai giraffe**

around the edges, extending down the entire lower leg. But the Thornicroft's giraffe (*Giraffa camelopardalis thornicrofti*), whose star-shaped or leafy spots extend to the lower leg, is seen only in the eastern part of Zambia.

It is prudent to remember that no one consulted the giraffes about these categories. All subspecies interbreed freely, and they can be very hard to differentiate. To complicate things further, some giraffes are born with no spots at all. Rare white specimens, perhaps albinos, have been documented in Tanzania, Uganda, and Kenya. Two solid beige babies were born to normally blotched parents in the Tokyo's Ueno Zoo, and a dark, almost black, bull

**Rare spotless tan giraffe**

roamed Serengeti. But they are the exceptions. Giraffes inherit their glorious spots at birth, and each is unique—like our fingerprints or the details of a snowflake—allowing researchers to use them to identify their subjects. One scien-

**Cape giraffe**

**Rothschild giraffe**

Camouflage

tist made a card catalog of 241 giraffe "neckprints."

What are the spots for? Rudyard Kipling took the traditional approach in a tale from his *Just So Stories* book, "How the Leopard Got His Spots." The giraffe, he wrote, started out "sandy-yellow-brownish all over" but hid from his enemies in a "great forest, 'sclusively full of trees and bushes and stripy, speckly, patchy-blatchy shadows . . . and what with standing half in the shade and half out of it, and what with the slippery-slidy shadows of the trees . . . the Giraffe grew blotchy. . . ." In other words, camouflage.

Another children's book calls it "giraffe magic," celebrating their ability to blend seamlessly into their surroundings. It is revealed to a calf named Ruva while still a youngster in Africa:

> *Ruva watched her aunts and uncles move in stately groups across the grassland. Sometimes they disappeared right before her eyes. One moment she saw a group of giraffes feeding at a tree. The next moment she saw a group of trees standing all together.*
> *"What happened to them?" she asked.*
> *"That is Giraffe Magic," said Mother. "You will learn it when you're older."*
> —Nancy Farmer,
> The Warm Place, 1995

It is a very neat trick, and it is astonishingly effective. "Though in the open the animals stand out like exclamation points on the landscape, in the sun-dappled shade of an acacia they melt into their surroundings, the spots on their long necks blending with the shadows on the bank," wrote a team of wildlife specialists in 1974. It also works in the shimmering heat of the midday sun, when these otherwise standout superstars seem to vaporize into the African ether. Countless hunters and tourists have stared indifferently at a weathered, decayed tree, only to realize the tree trunk is starting to move.

One half
of the giraffe
is neck.
The other half
is not.
Now, necks
that are a half of you
are really
quite a lot.
Although they let you
see afar
they're also
clearly spotted
(and even more
conspicuous
when they are
polka-dotted).

—Mary Ann
Hoberman, 1991

Some observers believed that the color and shape of the giraffe's spots coincided with the hue of its home. Thus the paler Nigerian giraffe was said to harmonize with its sandy Sahara habitat, while the richer-toned reticulated giraffe blended with its deeper bush. Another theory correlated skin color with the intensity of sunlight, those nearest the equator displaying the highest contrast between light and dark.

But others reject the notion of camouflage, saying the spots are for heat distribution. And anyway, there is no way to hide a giraffe. Even if they stand still, it is a dead giveaway when the tufted tail whisks at flies while the head peers about curiously. Theodore Roosevelt, who saw plenty of giraffes on safari despite his notorious nearsightedness, was adamant:

> Save under wholly exceptional circumstances no brute or human foe of the giraffe could possibly fail to see the huge creature if fairly close by; and at a distance the pattern of the colouration would be lost. The giraffe owes nothing to concealment; its colouration has not the slightest concealing effect so far as its foes are concerned.
> —Theodore Roosevelt, 1912

Maybe not. But it's sure fooled a lot of people.

# CHAPTER THREE

# The Inner Giraffe

I t is a very long way from giraffe hoof to brain, one-third of which is neck. All those years of evolution produced a marvel of engineering: seven gigantic vertebrae, ridged and grooved to hold a thick mass of muscle. And that's only the framework. Inside, scientists have long been intrigued with the cardiovascular implications of a head seven to ten feet higher than the heart. How does the giraffe pump blood all the way up to its brain? Even more critical, how—when the giraffe bends down nearly twenty feet to drink—does it prevent a fatal rush of blood into the cranial cavity and—when it raises the head up again—a dizzying depletion of blood?

"Sorry I'm late. . . .I had to gargle."

© 1996; reprinted courtesy of Bunny Hoest and Parade

Lunchtime, Samburu Game Reserve, Kenya

Since one cannot ask a giraffe to extend its arm for a blood pressure cuff, scientists had to devise some creative procedures to find the answers. First in the field, in 1955, was a team led by a South African physician, who darted the animals with curare, erected a steel scaffolding around them, then surgically implanted catheters into their carotid arteries with an instrument to take blood pressure readings. In the 1960s a U.S. team lassoed the giraffes, then inserted into each neck several instruments attached to a radio transmitter. The surgeries were brief, the instruments later removed, and the patients released successfully, unharmed.

What these hardy researchers discovered was a circulatory system exquisitely adapted to its peculiar shape. The giraffe's heart is an enormous two feet long and twenty-five pounds, with muscular walls several inches thick, driving the highest known blood pressure in any mammal: up to 280/180 mm Hg (millimeters of mercury) at heart level when prone, or more than twice that of ours. That would be a clear case of hypertension in humans, especially with a heart that beats up to 170 times a minute—also double our own. The secret of the giraffe's physiological equanimity lies in its blood vessels. The elastic walls of the lengthy carotid artery help force blood upward, then swell to absorb excess fluid when the head is lowered; in addition, each inch-wide-plus jugular vein contains a series of one-way valves that prevent backflow of the blood when the giraffe's head is down. When the head snaps back up, the pumping of the massive heart keeps blood flow constant. A plumber couldn't have designed it better.

Below the heart, the problem is the opposite: gravity easily pulls the blood six feet or so down to the tips of its hooves. But with nearly a ton or more of weight resting on four slim limbs, why doesn't the blood accumulate in the tissues around the extremities, giving the giraffe swollen ankles? When the animal is moving, contracting muscles help squeeze the blood into the veins. When the animal is still, yet another set of circulatory adaptations applies the pressure necessary to keep the blood flowing. Unlike the thin vessels near the brain, the arteries near the feet are thick walled and slightly less elastic, to decrease the downward blood pressure and keep them from ballooning. Arterial muscles also work hard to prevent fluid buildup in the feet. The final trick is the giraffe's skin. It fits so tightly on the animal's body that Dr. Alan Hargens (see box) calls it an "antigravity suit"—able to counteract the effects of gravity on giraffe limbs the way a test pilot's pressurized gear prevents blacking out in high altitudes.

# Giraffes in Space

Research into giraffe circulation may benefit future space flights. When astronauts reenter earth's atmosphere after extended space travel, they can black out. That's because blood vessels in their lower bodies lose tone during the days or weeks of weightlessness: they literally thin out. Then gravity draws down the blood, puffing up the ankles and depriving the brain. Dr. Alan Hargens, chief of the Gravitational Research Branch at NASA's Ames Research Center, has discovered that fetal giraffes, while suspended in a near weightless state in the uterus, also have thin blood vessels in their legs; but when they are born and enter the gravity field that is earth, the vessels start to thicken. Thus gravity may stimulate growth. He wants to give the astronauts what nature gave giraffes. So NASA is developing an artificial gravity machine for long-duration missions to prevent the weakening of the vascular system. He calls it a "negative pressure chamber"—a kind of waist-high vacuum cleaner that astronauts would enter to simulate earth's gravity field. They'd wear a new kind of suit, highly pressured at the abdomen but lower at the feet— to provide equal stress across the body and fool the arteries into maintaining their thick walls as they do on earth. Dr. Hargens says it's designed for prolonged travel aboard the space station or for a trip to Mars.

Perhaps the least understood feature of the giraffe's anatomy is its odd shape, which leads to its even odder gait. For centuries the sharp downward pitch of its back convinced observers that the front legs were much longer than the rear.

By 1820, British engraver Thomas Bewick realized that "the fore and hind legs are nearly of an equal height," but he repeated the three-hunded-year-old observation that "the shoulders rise so high that its back inclines like the roof of a house."

The resulting architecture has led to an astonishing method of locomotion. The giraffe walks with both legs on a side moving almost in tandem—in other words, right rear, then right front, then left rear, then left front—rather than with the diagonal gait of most quadrupeds. This technique, shared only by camels and pacing horses, serves an eminently practical purpose: to keep its long, stiltlike legs from getting entangled with one another. And it leads to the most unearthly image—a dreamy, eighteen-foot-tall obelisk solemnly and languidly drifting across the plains.

THE CAMELEOPARD.

Bewick

When the giraffe runs, or gallops, it is even more implausible. Now it moves its feet like a rabbit: two hind legs reaching outside of and beyond the two front, all the while pumping its neck to maintain speed and balance. The effect is pure magic, enabling it to achieve speeds up to thirty-five miles an hour. The swiftness of the animal was greatly appreciated by Arab hunters, whose highest praise to describe a horse was that it could catch a giraffe. While the pace cannot be maintained, it impresses everyone. The British hunter Cornwallis Harris was one of the first Europeans to witness the phenomenon:

> *Their motion, altogether, reminded me rather of the pitching of a ship, or rolling of a rocking-horse, than of any thing living; and the remarkable gait is rendered still more automa-*

*ton-like, by the switching, at regular intervals, of the*
*long black tail, which is invariably curled above the back, and*
*by the corresponding action of the neck, swinging as it does,*
*like a pendulum, and literally imparting to the animal the*
*appearance of a piece of machinery in motion.*
*—Capt. William Cornwallis Harris, 1844*

The sight of this apparent contradiction in physics has inspired a large assortment of images. Hunter Edgar Beecher Bronson in 1908 saw the "giraffe awkwardly side-wheeling along in giant strides and towering above the heaving mass like ambulant watch towers." Biologist J. Bristol Foster called the galloping giraffe "a paradigm of power, a kind of imperial grace." And nobody neglects the neck. It functions as a kind of mobile fulcrum, maneuvered to help propel the animal rising awkwardly from a sitting position or sailing over a fence. Kalman Kittenberger, who collected wildlife specimens for Hungary's National Museum in the early 1900s, compared its backward and forward motion to "the mast of a ship in a rough sea." Pioneering zookeeper Gerald Durrell saw them "dipping and swaying across the grass, their necks swinging from side to side like huge checkered pendulums." And an American adventurer in 1931 saluted their acrobatic skills:

*An interesting fact is that the long neck seems to take up*
*the motions of the body in such a way that it would be possi-*
*ble for a giraffe to carry a glass of water balanced between*
*his miniature horns without spilling a drop. The head*
*seems to float along on an even keel, while the rest of the*
*body wiggles all over.*
*—Paul L. Hoeffler, 1931*

Resting on that neck is one of the most endearing heads in the animal kingdom. The mouth is velvet soft and supple, with a hairy upper lip and a snakelike, purplish tongue nearly a foot and a half long. Atop the head are the knobby horns, or, more properly, ossicones, bumps of cartilage, covered with skin and hair, that start out as plates under the skin, then grow, ossify, and fuse to the skull. Both male and female giraffes have horns, but the bull has three, and they get larger and heavier as a result

of frequent head banging (see chapter 4). Some giraffes have five horns, for reasons not yet fully understood. There are only two ears, which are independently mobile.

**Portrait of a reticulated giraffe (left); eye of a Rothschild (above)**

Finally there are the eyes, which give the giraffe superb vision and give us the most exquisite pleasure. It is said that giraffes can spot a person more than a mile away, and one Africa hand claimed that giraffes on sentry duty would climb an anthill for the most unobstructed view. In 1959 a German scientist proved that giraffes can distinguish colors, picking out food from containers that were red, orange, yellow, yellow green, and violet.

But it is the aesthetic of the eye that appeals to us above all— its "bewitching softness," in the words of one converted hunter. I have gotten lost in a giraffe eye, too, mesmerized by the high gloss and sympathetic expression beneath those long, straight lashes. "There is nothing to compare with its beauty throughout the animal creation," wrote Sir Samuel Baker, who got to know giraffes after helping discover the source of the Nile.

A zoo curator I know, a bachelor, confessed to me with absolutely no embarrassment, "The day I find a woman with eyes as beautiful, I'll get married."

# THE FAR SIDE

By GARY

Giraffe beach parties

# Growing Up Giraffe

**G**iraffes are highly sociable creatures, whose gregarious nature has elicited centuries of respect. "It is extremely fond of society, and is very sensible," noted an appreciative Frenchman who captured two in 1836. "I have observed one of them shed tears when it no longer saw its companions, or the persons who were in the habit of attending to it."

A former San Diego Zoo curator called it their "laissez-faire approach to living":

> *There exists no less offensive a beast than the giraffe. It lives peaceably with its kind for the most part and bears not the slightest degree of ill-will toward other kinds of animals—both of which, as character recommendations, are more than can be said about the majority of people!*
> *—Ken Stott Jr. 1953*

Community life is a loosely knit herd that can include half a dozen or even many dozens of members. Naturalist Cynthia Moss listed the possibilities: "The groups may consist of males, females, and young, all males or all females, or any combination of sexes and ages. There is no consistency in the male/female ratio of a group or in the size of the groups. There are no obvious leaders in any case, and the group does not act as a coordinated unit." One researcher noted that adults of the same sex tend to hang out together—cows with cows, bulls with bulls; another said that in mixed groups, a middle-aged or older female tended to be the leader; yet another said there were no consistent leaders; and everyone has noticed that lone giraffes—male and female—can be seen.

They've also got plenty of friends. Giraffes can often be found with other animals—zebra, wildebeest, ostrich, eland—most of whom seem to rely on them as "living lookout towers":

*Once, visiting Kenya's Athi Plains, we witnessed the effectiveness of this tactic. From our car we could see giraffes, zebras, wildebeestes and hartebeests placidly feeding side by side. Sudddenly, an enormous bull giraffe snorted in alarm and broke into a gallop. Every one of the animals bolted and followed. A few hundred yards distant, they all stopped to look back: three hungry lionesses had risen from cover close*

**Herd of Rothschilds at Giraffe Manor**

*to the abandoned grazing site. Their game up, the big cats*
*headed into the bush to look elsewhere for dinner.*
      —*Emily and Ola D'Aulaire, wildlife writers, 1974*

Another African adventurer put it more imaginatively:

*The day before we left the water holes, we secured a moving*
*picture of no fewer than twelve giraffe. It took them nearly*
*two hours to come down to the water, but no sooner were they*
*there, when the other animals, perceiving them, abandoned*
*all their own cautious scouting and approaching, and came*
*fairly galloping down, helter-skelter, as if saying to them-*
*selves: "The giraffes are here, boys and girls, everything's*
*safe. Come on."*
                              —*James D. Barnes, 1915*

Giraffes also play host to a number of birds, most notably
the oxpeckers, or tick birds, who roam their enormous bodies
in search of ticks. While the oxpeckers are useful in removing
the bloodsuckers, they can also be a great annoyance, aggra-
vating wounds and irritating sensitive ears. In addition, black
piapiacs sometimes hitch a ride to snap up insects from the
surrounding airspace.

Immensely curious, incredibly friendly, and invariably
gentle, giraffes do have enemies. Number one is the two-
legged species –humans—who have hunted them for meat, or
pleasure, or trinkets, or merely driven them back by turning
grazing grounds into farmland. The ancestral threat, on a far
smaller scale, comes from the carnivores of the wild: mostly
lions, with a crocodile or cheetah or hyena very rarely making
the effort. Giraffes can—and do—fight back, with a lethal kick
from any of their mighty feet. Lions learn to keep their distance and attack wildebeests, zebras, and Thomson's gazelles
more often. Plenty of visitors to Africa's parks have witnessed
the perils faced by the king—make that queen—of the jungle.
It is, after all, the lioness who does most of the hunting and
killing:

*Time and again, though, I observed with what difficulty a lion*
*approaches the all-seeing giraffe. A herd of giraffes catching*

*sight of a lion commonly crane their necks to keep it under surveillance, even walking toward the predator to get a better view. A lion hesitates to attack prey that is aware it is being stalked.*

*Under direct threat of attack a giraffe generally beats a hasty retreat, although a female shepherding a small baby will stand her ground. Giraffes never employ their knobby horns against predators, but they can deliver a crushing blow with the hind foot, chop-kick with the forefoot like a horse, or strike with the whole stiff foreleg.*

*—J. Bristol Foster, biologist, 1977*


*A giraffe can kick in all four directions, and a hoof twelve inches wide, swung on a seven- or eight-foot shaft of heavy bone and muscle and backed by terrific driving power, can inflict a smashing blow and has been known to decapitate an over-anxious lioness.*

*Lions sometimes kill a full-grown giraffe, but it is only when they are hard-pressed by hunger and they can catch the giraffe at a disadvantage that they will make the attempt. A single lion is no match for a giraffe, but if two or more strike when the animal is reaching down to drink and has its legs spread wide apart, they have a good chance.*

*—George G. Goodwin, museum curator, 1956*


*It can happen, however, that a giraffe will shake off the attacker. I had good evidence of this when I saw a giraffe with its rump and haunches badly clawed. It was easy to figure out that the lion had jumped at it from behind but had been forced to let go, perhaps by the giraffe kicking out vigorously with its hind legs. The wounds had all healed well but the skin was deeply scarred and in places almost crumpled up.*

*—C. A. W. Guggisberg, author, 1969*

It would probably wound the lion further to learn that giraffe hooves are used purely for self-defense. They never kick each other.

Giraffes are most vulnerable when they are young, sick, or lying down, which explains why so few early explorers noticed them at rest. Some questioned whether giraffes ever slept, assuming their constant vigilance precluded the need to stretch out. In fact, they do doze off—the calf curled up on the ground with its neck gracefully tucked back over its rump, the grown-up resting at noon or at night, frequently while standing. But they never sleep more than a few minutes at a time, and they never stay down long, either. Consider this description from a century ago and you will wonder why they bother trying:

> *The actual process of lying down is a difficult one for the giraffe. Its neck leans gradually forward, like the mast of a barge being lowered, the hind-legs are bent under it, and the fore-legs doubled at the knees—rather in the manner of folding a flexible carpenter's rule.*
> —London Spectator, *1895*

Getting up is almost worse:

> *It throws its neck sharply backward, producing enough impetus to get its foreknees braced against the ground. Then a swing forward to roll the weight over the pivot and get the rear-end weight off the hind legs, enough to stretch them out and take a stance; followed by another vigorous backswing*

*of the neck to take the weight off the front end enough to*
*change the kneeling position to a standing one. Success!*
*And this all takes about a second and a half, which can mean*
*the affair is not a success at all if there is a lion about.*
                    —*Norman Meyers, wildlife photographer, 1972*

The lure of its flesh is a sad fate for a creature that carefully abstains from devouring others. Giraffes are vegetarians, feeding mostly on the leaves of the acacia, or thorn tree. Anyone who has been to Africa instantly recognizes the signature of the giraffe dining room: one level of the trees is sheared straight across, a permanent browse line that follows the herds like wilderness grafitti. Other trees can be turned into hourglass or cone shapes by their relentless feeding. And while researchers have confirmed that giraffes consume up to one hundred different species of plant life (sixty-six at one park alone), their favorite is the acacia, ranging from the whistling-thorn of Nairobi National Park to the *kameeldoring* (*Acacia giraffae*) named for them in South Africa. These flat-topped landmarks of the African skyline, with sharp spikes as long as a human thumb, would present a formidable challenge to a lesser creature. But the giraffe digs in with impunity—and great delicacy—grabbing the branch with its prehensile upper lip, then deftly winding its equally dextrous tongue around the main course. With sharp lower incisors, it combs the leaves off the branches, beginning a diges-

Giraffe tongue
(above)
and acacia leaves
guarded by thorns

**The flat-topped acacia in a rare break from nibbling giraffes**

tive process that can take most of the day.

Giraffes are ruminants, which means they have four-chambered stomachs and chew their cud. Author and animal expert Gerald Durrell found that activity particularly entertaining in his first zoo job, at England's Whipsnade Zoo, where he made the acquaintance of his first captive giraffe, a Baringo named Peter:

> *The only time Peter ever did anything which could be remotely described as vulgar was when he chewed the cud. He would stand contemplating me as I swept the floor of his house, his underjaw moving rhythmically from side to side; then he would swallow the mouthful and his jaw would become still, a glazed expression would spread over his face, and if you looked you would think that his mind was full of beautiful, poetical thoughts. He would have an air of waiting for something. At last it would come and it was so incongruous that it was almost laughable. Deep in the poet's stomach you could hear a curious rumbling which ended in a sort of pop. A ball of food would make its appearance at the base of his long neck and, bulging the skin as it went, would travel upward with all the majesty of a department-*

*store lift. The ball was generally about the size of a coconut,
and it would end its travels by rolling into his mouth. A
satisfied expression would replace the look of thoughtful
genius, and Peter's lower jaw would recommence its monot-
onous movement. I could never make out whether he could
control the supply of food. If he could not, I fear it must be
embarrassing in the wild state to have, say, one's declara-
tion of love suddenly interrupted by this loud and stately
regurgitation of one's breakfast.*

*—Gerald Durrell, 1973*

To fuel their immense bodies, giraffes consume seventy-
five pounds of vegetation each day. In a neat closing of the
ecological circle, their browsing stimulates new growth and
thus helps propagate the very plants they consume. In addition, some seeds need to pass through their digestive system
before they can regenerate in the soil. This public-spirited
penchant to recycle is matched only by their generous nature
at the dining table. Giraffes readily share their branches with
their peers, a trait that earned the approval of Anne Innis
Dagg during her research in Sydney, Australia.

*The tolerance of giraffe for each other contrasted greatly
with the behavior of other ungulates at the Taronga Zoo.
In the breeding season many of these males have to be sepa-
rated. When this had not been done earlier, fighting had
caused . . . death . . . and injury. . . . Even female ungulates
were sometimes intolerant of each other . . . [refusing] to
allow subordinate individuals to have their share of the food.
What an admirable example is set by the gentle giraffe.*

*—Anne Innes Dagg and J. Bristol Foster, 1976*

There is controversy over the giraffe's need for water,
largely because they get so much fluid from greenery. One
person says they drink ten gallons on a hot day; another measured two gallons a week. A scientist in Namibia observed
populations of Angola giraffes in the desert regions of Etosha
National Park that he says never drink. In the zoo they drink
up heartily. In the wild, when they do get thirsty, they exer-
cise the greatest caution at the watering hole, because of their

Critic Jay Jacobs once reviewed the New York restaurant Girafe, whose northern Italian cuisine and angular, life-size metallic statue of the animal inspired this bit of whimsy:

*Too long and thin by more than half is*
*What the neck of the giraffe is.*
*A question I find very hard is*
*How the beast camelopardis*
*Somehow managed to forget he*
*Was born to feed upon spaghetti.*

*Unlike the hippo or the goat, he*
*Is quite exceptionally throaty;*
*With two yards from his chest to chin, he*
*Should favor foodstuffs long and skinny;*
*That's logical, I think, and yet he*
*Has not experienced trenette.*

*Set mule-like in his stubborn ways, he*
*Shuns tagliatelle bolognese;*
*He's never even tried linguine,*
*Nor has he eaten fettucini,*
*Nor stuffed his neck (and then his belly)*
*With any sort of vermicelli.*

*It seems the dumb giraffe believes he*
*Daintily must nibble leaves; he*
*Dines on trees and trees alone; he*
*Has no urge for macaroni,*
*Be it suavely sauced capelli*
*D'angelo or perciatelli.*
*—Jay Jacobs, 1981*

vulnerability when bending down.

What's it like to grow up as a giraffe? Start with the fact that it begins abruptly. After fifteen months in the womb, babies, or calves, are born headfirst and dropped six feet to the ground from the standing mom. Boom. Welcome to earth. The calf itself weighs close to 150 pounds and measures almost six feet tall; it is usually up on its own spindly legs within an hour, a vital defense against a hungry enemy. An American tourist riding horseback in Kenya's Lewa Downs inadvertently frightened a newborn still in the process of being licked clean by its mother. As the cow took off, the calf wheeled and clumsily jogged after her, a decidedly grand accomplishment after just a few minutes out of the womb. Even so, predators (and disease) claim about 75 percent of all babies within the first year.

The youngsters who do survive—almost always single calves, as twins are very rare—grow rapidly, as much as six feet in the first year. And they are captivating.

> *A baby giraffe is one of the most delightful of the young ungulates. In proportion to its size, the mane on the back of the neck appears bigger than in the adult and the head is prettily adorned by two tassels marking the position of the horns. The neck is carried very upright, slightly bent in the shape of an S, and this, added to their independent behaviour, gives young giraffes a very self-possessed air.*
> *—C. A. W. Guggisberg, author, 1969*

During one of their long sojourns in East Africa, photographers Martin and Osa Johnson encountered a tiny, fawn-colored newborn lying at the feet of its mom.

> *We did not attempt to take pictures of the two giraffes, but merely watched them from a distance for a long time. The mother giraffe stood there gazing at us with an appealing, helpless expression in her puzzled, brown eyes. She couldn't run away and desert the baby, and she was afraid of us two strange beings.*
>
> *She stood so silently, with her head high in the air, listening for sounds of peril. Now and then she snuggled her nose against the baby at her feet and gently nudged him. Then slowly that great neck would sweep upward. With ears erect, nostrils distended, she stood, watchful, alert, and nervous. We left the mother and her baby when the little fellow was just beginning to struggle to his feet.*

*[She later encounters the pair again, the baby toddling in its mother's wake.]*

*His lips stood out, and he kept rubbing against his mother's legs. Evidently he was hungry, but his mother nudged him away with her head. Once she gave him a hard push that nearly knocked him off his feet.*

*The big giraffe neared the water slowly, looking carefully about in fear that her age-old enemy, the lion, might be lurking near by. A mischievous breeze finally tossed my scent in her direction. She stood still and looked directly at me with an expression of surprise. Then she turned and galloped away . . . [the baby] following with awkward little jumps. . . .*

—Osa Johnson, 1930

**Osa Johnson and guide greet a newborn**

Giraffe babies, with their brushlike manes, tassels for horns, and S-curved necks, are so fetching, the whole herd seems to dote on them. Conservation pioneer Bernhard Grzimek described a birth at South Africa's Kruger National Park, where "no less than nine giraffes formed a circle round the expectant mother." As the calf struggled to stand up—falling at first, tottering about— it finally walked "and seemed quite strong. All the other giraffes bent to nuzzle the new addition to the herd."

Giraffe cows themselves are terrific moms, but it took years to unearth that behavior. Dr. Vaughan A. Langman, now a physiology professor at Louisiana State University, studied them for seven years, outfitting giraffes with fiberglass collars that were cushioned by pieces of horse blanket and embedded with radio transmitters. His goal was to uncover the secret that had eluded many researchers:

**Margaret III, Bronx Zoo, 1994**

Why did some giraffe mothers seem to neglect their babies? Why weren't they seen spending time with them? Dr. Langman learned that like some other mammals, they were hiding them:

> *Immediately after birth, the giraffe cow moves her calf a short distance to an area of safety. Here the calf is completely isolated from all other giraffes for a period which may last as long as a month. During this time, the calf stays in the area, lying down and moving very little. The cow returns two to three times a day to allow the calf to nurse. She may go up to 15 miles away from the hidden calf for water or food. The calf waits for her to return. . . .*
>
> *Over an extended period they hide their young in groups and provide "baby-sitting" services.*
>
> *During the early morning, the giraffe cows with their calves will move to special areas that are used repeatedly by nursery herds. They all eat together for a while, and then the cows leave one by one. Soon only the calves remain; they lie down and nibble trees very near to where they were left. Two or three times during the day each cow returns to the nursery group and lets her calf suckle. The cows will then leave again, but at the end of the day return and stay with their calves to protect them during the night.*
>
> *At night the nursery herd maintains one or two giraffes as watchmen to ensure that lions cannot approach unnoticed. They change watch regularly so that no giraffe is on duty all night. This is accomplished without a sound and without any apparent plan. . . .*
>
> *Next morning all of the giraffes travel to an area similar to one where the calves were left the day before; and just as before, the cows begin to leave their calves and travel to feeding areas. However, this time not all the giraffe cows leave; one mother remains behind with all the other calves. Yesterday's hidden group of calves becomes a calf pool with one mother as the baby-sitter. How that giraffe cow becomes sitter for the day is not clear. At first glance it seems so planned that you think each cow takes turns. It is more likely that the baby-sitting cow feels no urge to drink or seek out special feeding areas and simply stays behind because she lacks a motive for leaving.*
>
> —Dr. Vaughan A. Langman, 1982

Dr. Langman says this baby-sitting system also serves as an air conditioner, screening the calves from the heat of the African day until their bodies are large enough to deal with it. It safeguards the lives of the babies, too, since one mom perceiving a predator and nudging her own calf to flee will alert the entire nursery to danger.

Even in captivity, giraffe moms take their jobs seriously. The mother of a two-week-old calf I visited in Florida was alert the entire day I was there, cautiously standing between her daughter and myself lest I produce something more threatening than a camera.

The giraffe cow's ferocious ability to protect her baby is well documented. In 1982 a tourist to Kenya's Masai Mara Game Reserve watched one giraffe mother trying to defend her two-week-old baby from a pride of lions. The calf had been attacked and was bleeding from the neck. As its mother urged it to stand, and to follow her away, it wobbled and sank to the ground. With the lions circling closer, Mom "wheeled in a flash, head down and hooves flailing. She charged right into the lions and kicked them off." The drama took an hour to play out. Finally the baby collapsed and "the mother was still wandering disconsolately about the feasting lions."

Adolescence presents a whole new set of problems, depending on gender. Females are sexually mature after about four years, males at three and a half. But you can tell the boys from the girls far sooner than that. Young bulls engage early in a ritual called "necking." Do

Mom watching me warily while guarding her baby

not confuse this with its human counterpart. Giraffe "necking"—a term first applied by researcher Anne Innis Dagg in 1958—bears no resemblance to lovemaking, serving instead as a form of play fighting or even serious combat that entails swinging their necks at each other and striking body blows with the head. Most of the time these slow-motion, boyish battles are utterly benign "sparring matches," with the participants squaring off—either nose to nose or nose to tail—and rubbing

**Giraffe bulls "necking"**

or batting or even entwining their necks for an hour or so. I have seen them draw arches in the air, then drift off.

> *The blows are almost always delivered gently, in the tempo of a stately dance, there are sometimes long pauses, and when they stop sparring they are likely to browse side-by-side. . . .*
>
> *The behaviour of both animals suggests play much more than fighting. . . . This play provides practice in an activity that may, in later life, be used in fighting to determine the right to breed.*
>
> —David M. Pratt and Virginia H. Anderson,
> researchers, 1985

In other words, these are practice dominance matches, preparing the animal for the day when it may use the sledgehammer force of the flexible club that is its neck with the added weapon of its bone-hard horns, to defeat and outrank another bull. The real fights can be terrifying.

*We watched, once, as two big bulls in Kenya's Amboseli Game Reserve stopped their browsing at some inner signal and, legs stiffened, squared off flank to flank. They began to swing their long necks upward and back over their shoulders in a wide arc. At first each avoided the blow of the other and the rhythmic alternation of strike and dodge gave the battle the appearance of a ritual dance. Then the blows struck on target and heads slammed against necks and sides with resounding thuds. A male's head can weigh 24 pounds, three times that of the nonfighting female, and the force of one of these blows may lift an opponent clear off his feet. Like their running, however, this too seemed slow-motion, down to the golden billows of dust raised by the shuffling hooves. The battle ended when one of the two decided he'd had enough and ambled off a few paces. The victor did not give chase and, as we left the herd, the two had resumed their casual browsing.*
—Emily and Ola D'Aulaire, wildlife writers, 1974

*In Kenya's Masai Mara Game Reserve, two adult males, set in battle, slugged each other so hard that sickening bone-crunching "thuds" resounded across the plains, and the impacts lifted the one-and-a-half-ton animals off their feet. Although sinus cavities fill a giraffe's head, an additional 20 pounds of bone form on the top of the skull throughout the animal's life to transform the head, with its rounded horns, into a titanic armored weapon. The battle ended when one male walked away. He forded a narrow, shallow river and dropped dead on the other bank, presumably from internal injuries.*
—Jane Stevens, science writer, 1993

*The rivals take up position side by side, often facing the same way but not infrequently looking in opposite directions, holding their heads high in a threat gesture. Then one of them bends his neck outwards and swings back, smashing the head against the shoulder of the other bull with such force that the "plonk" can be heard at quite a distance. . . . The second bull replies by swinging his neck in a wide arch, scoring a thudding blow worthy of Thor's hammer. As the bout con-*

*tinues, the swipes become more violent and the duellists spread their forelegs in order to keep their balance. With horns turned sideways they batter the other's chest, rump and flank mercilessly, the blows tending to land lower and lower as the fight gathers momentum and the two contestants slowly rotate around a common axis. . . .*

*The fight may continue with a few short breathing spells for a quarter of an hour or twenty minutes; then it suddenly fizzles out with one or other of the bulls jumping aside with a few cantering steps, or simply walking out of the "ring," as if nothing had happened. It is often quite difficult to decide which one of the two actually won the match. . . .*

—*C. A. W. Guggisberg, author, 1969*

*Like the males of other species, the giraffe bull's main goal is to pass on his genetic material. In order to fulfull this goal he must work his way up through the rank order until he is in a position to court and mate with a female without undue intereference from other males. Fights are rare, because there is usually one dominant male around whom the other males will not challenge.*

—*Cynthia Moss, naturalist, 1982*

Courtship itself seems a far less passionate affair, although males on the make are determined. When one approaches a group of females, he checks to see if she is in estrus, or heat, a one-day event that occurs every two weeks or so. He nuzzles her rear, stimulating her to urinate, then takes a sample, lifts his head, and curls back his lips—a grotesque-looking procedure known as "flehman." If she is not available, the suitor turns away; if she is, he hangs out with dogged zeal and a real sense of possession.

*If other bulls are present, they watch with keen interest but keep out of the way. Active courtship may go on for one or two days, interspersed with hour-long periods in which the participants browse side by side. In time, the bull stands close at her rump, moves his hind feet forward to touch her hind leg . . . and, sliding his forelegs up along her flanks, he tries to mount. She usually thwarts this attempt by walk-*

*ing forward. At last she may stand for him; he mounts, makes three or four vigorous thrusts, the last of which brings his head and neck into a position so nearly upright that he seems to be about to fall over backwards, and in a moment they have both returned to browsing.*
*—David M. Pratt and Virginia H. Anderson,*
*researchers, 1985*

Pratt, a biologist, and Anderson, a psychotherapist, also found that age is as important to giraffe romance as it is to humans. They found that cows tend to prefer older bulls; that older bulls were more attentive than younger ones; and that bulls were most interested in young cows, although middle-aged cows were preferred to old cows. The researchers concluded that "sexual competition favours older males and younger females," a finding that could give new meaning to the term "trophy giraffe."

Whatever her age, the cow then begins one of the longest pregnancies in the animal world—about fifteen months—a condition that is still difficult for humans to detect. Cows bear their first calf when they are about five years old, and have been known to deliver up to ten babies over the course of a lifetime.

In the wild, cows tend to wander off to find a secluded spot for the blessed event, but giraffes in captivity are permitted no such privacy. One experiment, designed with an eye to long-term survival in captivity, tried to determine if giraffes and okapis could carry each other's offspring in utero. The finding was negative, meaning we will not see giraffe surrogate moms.

Finally, their brains. Are giraffes smart? Does it matter? It has been suggested that they may communicate with their necks and tails, in a kind of mammalian semaphore system. Or

**Giraffes mating**

that they may use ultrasonics, a high-pitched signal, to contact each other. Betty Leslie-Melville, who adopted two giraffes at her home in Kenya (see chapter 7), thought something was transpiring when a newly captured calf stood facing the brick wall at the rear of its enclosure throughout the evening. Not a sound was uttered, not a motion detected. But its mother waited just outside the same wall all night long . . . and then walked away.

Leslie-Melville also says that Daisy, one of their guests, logically figured out a way to extricate herself from the sloping sides of their fishpond—an especially resourceful feat since giraffes cannot swim.

Then there's naturalist James L. Clark, who helped set up the exhibits for the American Museum of Natural History. He tried in vain to shoot at a herd of giraffe, only to find them outwitting him day after day. He plotted and tried to trick them, but they constantly walked just out of his range. After four days of frustration, he gave it one more go:

*But now my dander was up! I was determined. There wasn't a giraffe in Africa that could outwit me indefinitely—or so I thought. [He lines up four men to direct the giraffes toward him. Foiled again.] Instead, they galloped along within fifty yards or a little more of that whole string of natives, as if they knew perfectly that they were in no danger from them, and finally, having passed in review before my whole line of sentinels, and having passed at a good two hundred and fifty yards from where I was swearing at them under my breath, they swung around the end man and made their way directly to the knoll upon which they invariably spent each day.*

*At that I gave up.*

*—James L. Clark, 1928*

# CHAPTER FIVE

# "Praise Be to Thee, Lord, for Sister Giraffe"

"**N**o one who has merely seen the giraffe in a cold climate can form the least idea of its beauty in its native land," wrote a nineteenth-century explorer after his first trip to Africa. A fellow Briton added, "The spectacle of a troop of wild giraffe is certainly one of the most wonderful things in nature. The uncommon shape, the great height, the long, slouching stride, the slender necks, reaching hither and thither among the spreading leafage of the camel-thorn trees, the rich colouring of the animals— all these things combine to render the first meeting with the giraffes in

Oh good and glorious giraffe,
I'd like to speak in your behalf.
It's clear that there are very few
Who decorate the world like you.
—Johannes Eff, 1969

**Sunset, South Africa**

their native haunts one of the most striking and memorable of experiences."

In their native habitat, giraffes are frequently richer in color and more alert than their tamed cousins. I think they are like palm trees: seen one by one, transplanted and plunked onto a highway, palms have always struck me as grand but ungainly misfits. But viewed by the hundreds at home in their desert oasis, they are glorious. It's the same with giraffes.

In his dictionary of 1755, Dr. Samuel Johnson, who had never met one, defined the giraffe as an "Abyssinian animal, taller than an elephant, but not so thick." Subsequent writers, enjoying the distinct advantage of having seen their subject, made more poetic comparisons.

> *Out on the Safaris . . . I had time after time watched the progression across the plain of the Giraffe, in their queer, inimitable, vegetative gracefulness, as if it were not a herd of animals but a family of rare, long-stemmed, speckled gigantic flowers slowly advancing.*
> —Isak Dinesen, Out of Africa, *1937*

> *Praise be to thee, Lord, for Sister Giraffe, the which is an ambler, full of grace, exceedingly demure and absent-minded, and carries her small head high above the grass, with long lashes to her veiled eyes, and which is so much a lady that one refrains from thinking of her legs, but remembers her as floating over the plain in long garbs, draperies of morning mist or mirage.*
> —Isak Dinesen, Shadows on the Grass, *1960*

> *[As the hunter watches, a herd of nine giraffes emerges from the bush.] Their lofty heads and necks much the color of the surrounding bush, above which they towered before entering the open, the impressing of their approach was quite as startling as if one were to see the Singer, St. Paul and Manhattan Life Buildings strolling, Indian file, up Fifth Avenue. . . . [N]ot one moved until I entered the open—and*

**Masai giraffe**

*then they lurched away, at about as graceful a pace as one
might expect of the Singer Building out on stilts.*
                    —*Edgar Beecher Bronson, American hunter, 1910*

*It is just a great mass of swaying, surging life, topped by long
necks, and borne along with seven-league strides, apparently
ever in each other's way, yet never fouling, never slackening
speed. And what a play of color there is! The old bull, as he
runs neck and neck with two fawn-coloured cows, looks black as
a raven's plume. A brilliant chestnut cow crosses him; without
check he swings to the right, and at once the deep black becomes
richest blowing orange-brown: then as he strides out half-left—
after passing with graceful sweep of his great neck under the
clustering branches of a widespreading thorn-tree, close to
which he has had to run to avoid trampling a half-grown thing
that has been striving to keep pace with one of the older cows,
doubtless its mother—he heads his two former companions, and
the glancing sunlight flashes over him and robes him in silver
sheen. Such toning, mingling, and changing of colours—the
eye is dazzled with their wonderful beauty!*
—*Frederick Vaughan Kirby, British hunter and journalist, 1896*

*I often think of them still—moving about like phantoms
among the thorny bushes, and in and out the sunlit woods,
or standing out silhouetted against the horizon.*
                                        —*C. G. Schillings,
                    German wildlife photographer and hunter, 1907*

*A giraffe swaying across the horizon at sunset is as serene
and graceful as it was at noontime when it moved across the
heat-haze mirage as if it were walking on water.*
                    —*Norman Meyers, wildlife photographer, 1972*

*It is a strange sight, which lends a touch of magic to the effect
of the soft evening light upon the veld, as they reappear into
the open and are sharply set off against the skyline. These
extraordinary ruminants are, indeed, an ornament to the
locality they inhabit. Stalking with dignified pace they
travel obliquely across the plain, slowly fading away in the
distance. Such a sight, once witnessed, lingers in the mind of*

*the fascinated observer. The charm of the African veld casts*
*a curious spell over a wanderer, rarely ever to release its grip,*
*and creates in him a longing to return to its mystic beauty.*
                              *—Marius Maxwell, photographer, 1925*

*It is always worth pausing to watch a giraffe, whatever the*
*time and whatever it is doing. There it is, this phenomenon,*
*right before your eyes, a marvel of adaptive forces, just* there.
                              *—Norman Meyers, 1972*

When Osa Johnson laid eyes on her first giraffe, while on
a train traveling to Mombasa from Nairobi, she found it "a
strange, misshapen beast that caused me much wonder."

*Some jokester must have stolen into the workshop of life to*
*build this droll creature, using an assortment of odds and*
*ends that were left over. The body resembled that of a camel*
*modeled by an impatient schoolboy. It was mounted on four*
*long, slender legs that looked like stilts. The neck was a*
*masterpiece of absurdity. It stretched away from the shoul-*

Reticulated parade, Samburu Game Reserve, Kenya

*ders as though it were made of taffy and had been pulled by
some playful urchin. On top of the neck was a head, small and
insignificant in comparison to the rest of the animal. It was
decked with two tiny horns just about big enough to hang a
hat on. Two round ears protruded curiously from the sides.*

*His coat was a reddish brown embroidered with an oak-
leaf pattern of black. At the stern he wore a long, slim tail
decorated with a tassel of black hair.*

*My first impulse was to laugh at that big giraffe, but I
felt friendly toward him, too. He was a dignified-looking
beast, despite his grotesque build. His head was about on a
level with the top of the train. I worried a little for fear he
would get tangled up in the telegraph wires that bordered
the railroad and choke himself to death.*

*The funny fellow looked at me with warm, friendly eyes
and nodded his head as though to bid me good-morning.
The impression was so vivid that I nodded back and thought,
"Hello, yourself."*

*The giraffe didn't seem to be afraid. He stood there and
surveyed the train calmly as it passed, making no gesture of
retreat. As he faded into the distance, it occurred to me of a
sudden that something was missing from that picture. That
giraffe should have been wearing a high silk hat.*

—Osa Johnson, *explorer and photographer, 1930*

Fred Astaire couldn't have looked more elegant. Gerald
Durrell, who would meet and care for hundreds of different
species at the zoo he created on the Channel Island Jersey, was
an early convert. Here begins his love affair with the zoo
giraffe named Peter:

*It was while I was feeding Billy sugar lumps that Peter
decided to move. He swallowed the last bit of hay and then*

*came pacing down the length of the house toward me. It was really rather eerie; one got the same sense of unreality one would get—the same shock—if one suddenly saw a tree uproot itself and drift across the landscape. For Peter did drift. The mechanism that controlled those vast limbs was incredible, for here was the tallest mammal on earth coming toward me and yet he moved as casually and as gracefully as a deer and as silently as a cloud. He was not ungainly; he was completely unhurried, and his beauty of movement did not allow you to notice his disproportionate limbs or his great height. Giraffes are, after all, built for clumsiness, but there was no ugliness here. He came to a stop some twelve feet away from me, by which time his head was directly above me, and then slowly lowered his head and peered into my face. The length and thickness of his eyelashes had to be seen to be believed, as did the liquid beauty of his enormous dark eyes gazing at me with a spirit of gentle inquiry. He sniffed at me with the utmost delicacy and politeness. Then, having apparently decided that I was harmless, he turned and sauntered off. His tail was a long, sweeping pendulum of ivory silk hair and he swished it gently from side to side; his complicated pattern of honey-brown and cream was a unique and beautiful mosaic. From that moment on, Peter and, indeed, every giraffe that ever lived had me under its spell.*

—Gerald Durrell, 1973

As adoptive giraffe mom Betty Leslie-Melville noted:

*A giraffe is unbelievably beautiful, it has liquid eyes and film-star-lashes, it is gentle and graceful and it doesn't bother anyone.*

—Betty Leslie-Melville, 1977

# WILD SPORT
OF
## Southern Africa.

W.C. Harris.

# CHAPTER SIX

# Hunting the Giraffe

**M**aybe it was battle fatigue from fighting the Republican revolution. Maybe it was the documentary on Africa he'd just seen on TV. Or maybe Newt Gingrich, the newly elected Speaker of the House of Representatives, really meant it when he told his "Renewing American Civilization" class at Georgia's Reinhardt College that the difference between men and women was the giraffe. No kidding. It was January 1995, and the subject was battlefield combat—specifically, which sex was better suited.

*If combat means being in a ditch, females have biological problems staying in a ditch for thirty days because they get infections, and they don't have upper body strength. I mean, some do,*

Frontispiece to Capt. Harris' book (see page 89)

*but they're relatively rare. . . . On the other hand, if com-*
*bat means being on an Aegis-class cruiser managing the*
*computer controls for twelve ships and their rockets, a*
*female . . . may be dramatically better than a male who gets*
*very, very frustrated sitting in a chair all the time because*
*males are biologically driven to go out and hunt giraffes.*
—Newt Gingrich, Speaker of the House, 1995

The Speaker's startling choice of prey and his curious version of biology touched off a round of bemused commentary
inside the Beltway. A Democratic congressman who showed
up late for a vote explained that he had driven by the National
Zoo and gotten "this incredible urge to hunt giraffes. So I
pulled in and drove to their cage." A TV critic suggested that
giraffe tartare might be on the menu at the Gingrich home.
And a weekly contest in *The Washington Post* asking for "coun-
try-western song titles on the general subjects of Lovin',
Cheatin', Thievin', Drinkin', Truckin', or Dogs," awarded
honorable mention to the entry "You Left Me in a Ditch, Bro-
kenhearted and Infected, You Giraffe-Hunting Bastard."

Political cartoonist Pat Oliphant saw things this way:

Colorado congresswoman Pat Schroeder took
the issue to the floor of the House. With a bewildered look
on her face and a twinkle in her eye, she said she was "very,
very troubled by the new factual data that seems to be coming

out of our new leader. . . . Now I have been working in a male culture for a very long time," she went on, trying hard not to smile, "and I have not met the first one who wants to go out and hunt a giraffe."

Nor have I, but that's only because we live in enlightened times. Just one hundred years ago giraffes were prime quarry, and Speaker Gingrich certainly got the gender right. It is men, not women, who have hunted giraffes through the ages. "The connection of hunting with masculinity runs deep," writes Matt Cartmill in a penetrating book on the subject. "Hunting has been a stereotypically male activity throughout most of Western history." The only females I found who kill giraffes are lions (see chapter 4), and that's about survival, not sex.

In the human world it was primitive men, not their wives, who trapped and speared and shot giraffes with bows and arrows. Nubian men from a tribe called the Aggageers used knives. An 1878 issue of *Frank Leslie's Popular Monthly*, with jour-

Engraving of the Aggageers, 1878, was accompanied by this explanation: "Our readers will see in our illustration an exciting episode of a giraffe chase; all the particulars of the dress, etc., were drawn most faithfully on the spot by a traveling artist, Mr. R. Hartmann."

nalist-explorer Henry Stanley on the cover, featured an eyewitness account of nearly nude Africans and Bedouin males riding bareback on swift camels. Each wore a "long and broad cross-hilted sword, sheathed in a reddish-colored leather scabbard" slung over his left shoulder. After a frantic chase across the dusty plains, the execution was speedy:

> *When the hunter has arrived at a sufficiently short distance, he leans forward on his seat, takes aim, and with his ponderous sword hamstrings his victim. Rarely is a second blow*

*needed to fell the colossal frame of the pursued giraffe. The
animal falls panting into the grass, or crouches down upon
its hind legs in convulsions, and kicks to right and left,
whirling up clouds of dust. . . .*

*[The swordsmen] dismount from their dromedaries and
dispatch the victim by a few sword-cuts into the throat and
the extremities.*

—Frank Leslie's Popular Monthly, *1878*

Encouraged by such derring-do, men from Europe and
America avidly saddled up. More than a century of popular
literature written by, and paying homage to, the Great White
Hunters, venerates the so-called glory and gallantry of those
who rode to kill the gentle giraffes. For these iron men of the
past who charged into the veld or the bush in their kilts and
turbans, chasing down giraffes with a favored rifle was the ultimate sporting adventure. Those who justify their zeal remind
us that public attitudes were different back then; that hunters
have always been among the most environmentally aware,
combining their love of the chase with deep respect for nature.

We are also told that the hunt, like no other activity, makes
a man really feel like a man.

François LeVaillant was a French naturalist who made two
pioneering trips to South Africa in the 1780s. His goal was worthy—to expand scientific understanding of this rare species. But
his enthusiasm for the kill is jarring. We join him midpursuit:

*Instantly, ravished with joy, I leaped on one of my horses,
made Bernfry mount another, and, attended by my dogs,
hastened towards the mimosa. The giraffe was not there;
but we saw him crossing the plain towards the west, and we
spurred on our horses to overtake him. He trotted on lightly
without exerting himself in the least, while we galloped
after, firing occasionally at him; however, he insensibly
gained upon us, so that after a chase of three hours, our
horses being completely out of breath, we were obliged to
stop, and soon lost sight of him. . . .*

*[Later he kills one giraffe with a single shot.]*

*Who would believe that such a conquest should excite
transports in my mind bordering on madness? Troubles,*

*fatigues, pressing wants, uncertainty of the future, and sometimes disgust of the past, disappeared together: all fled at the sight of this new prize. I could not satisfy my eyes with contemplating it. I measured its immense height. My eyes turned with astonishment from the animal destroyed to the instrument of destruction. . . . I was the first to kill this; and with this I was about to enrich natural history; I was about to destroy romance and establish a truth in my turn.*
*—François LeVaillant, 1796*

**Captain William Cornwallis Harris, "Hunting the Giraffe," 1844**

LeVaillant was not the first to sacrifice a giraffe for science (see chapter 1), but his ardor was infectious. Captain William Cornwallis Harris, whose reverence for the animal has already been noted, read LeVaillant as a child and dreamed of "the slender and swan-like neck of the stately giraffe, bowing distantly to our better acquaintance." After serving in India as an officer in the Bombay Engineers, he ached to ride in Africa, later confessing, "From my boyhood upwards, I have been taxed by the facetious with *shooting-madness,* and truly a most delightful mania I have ever found it." In fairness, Harris tempered his blood lust with naturalism, painting wonderful watercolors of the South African fauna. But in a book about his experiences—the first on African game—he also devoted a huge segment to the conquest. His romantic prose and poetry typifies the often exaggerated bravado of the genre.

*Well do I recall the avidity with which, in the days of my boyhood, I devoured Le Vaillant's picturesque and eloquent account of his first success in the chase of the Giraffe, at a period when men had long doubted of its existence; and*

*many a time has my own bosom since leapt to the very emo-*
*tions he describes. The appearance of a troop of those ante-*
*diluvian figures, gliding majestically amid the wild*
*magnificence of an African landscape, never failed to trans-*
*port me beyond myself. . . .*

*It was on the morning after our departure from the res-*
*idence of his Amazooloo Majesty that I first actually saw the*
*Giraffe. . . . [A]n object which had repeatedly attracted my*
*eye — but which I had as often persuaded myself was noth-*
*ing more than the branchless stump of some withered tree,*
*suddenly shifted its position, and the next moment I dis-*
*tinctly perceived that singular form, of which the appari-*
*tion had oftimes visited my slumbers—but upon whose*
*reality I now gazed for the first time. Gliding rapidly*
*among the trees, above the topmost branches of many of*
*which its graceful head nodded like some lofty pine, all doubt*
*was in another moment at an end—it was the stately, the*
*long-sought-for Giraffe. Putting spurs to my horse, and*
*directing the Hottentots to follow, I presently found myself*
*half choked with excitement, rattling at the heels of an ani-*
*mal which to me had been a stranger even in its captive*
*state, and which thus to meet, free on its native plains, has*
*fallen to the lot of but few of the votaries of the chase. Sail-*
*ing before me with incredible velocity, his long swan-like*
*neck keeping time to the eccentric motion of his stilt-like*
*legs—his ample black tail curled above his back, and whisk-*
*ing in ludicrous concert with the rocking of his dispropor-*
*tioned frame, he glided gallantly along "like some tall ship*
*upon the ocean's bosom," and seemed to leave whole leagues*
*behind him at each stride.*

*[He gives chase and fires twice, but the giraffe escapes.*
*Several days later, he comes across 32 members of a herd.]*

*My heart leapt within me, and the blood coursed like*
*quicksilver through my veins, for, with a firm wooded plain*
*before me, I knew that they were mine. . . .*

*[He shoots.]*
*The lordly chief, being readily distinguishable from the rest*
*by his dark chestnut robe and superior stature, I applied the*
*muzzle of my rifle behind his dappled shoulder with the*
*right hand, and drew both triggers; but he still continued to*

*shuffle along, and being afraid of losing him, should I dismount . . . I sat in my saddle, loading and firing behind the elbow, and then placing myself across his path, to obstruct his progress. Mute, dignified, and majestic stood the unfortunate victim, occasionally stooping his elastic neck towards his persecutor, the tears trickling from the lashes of his dark humid eye, as broadside after broadside was poured into his brawny front. . . .*

*Presently a convulsive shivering seized his limbs—his coat stood on end—his lofty form began to totter—and at the seventeenth discharge from the deadly grooved bore, like a falling minaret, bowing his graceful head from the skies, his proud form was prostrate in the dust. Never shall I forget the intoxicating excitement of that moment! At last, then, the summit of my hunting ambition was actually attained, and the towering Giraffe laid low. Tossing my turbanless cap into the air—alone, in the wild wood, I hurraed with bursting exultation, and unsaddling my steed, sank exhausted with delight beside the noble prize that I had won.*

*—Capt. William Cornwallis Harris, 1840*

Captain Harris' account illustrates the conflict faced by many hunters: the minute they saw their prey up close, they underwent a change of heart, however brief. This schizophrenic attitude was shared by Roualeyn Gordon Cumming of Scotland, who spent five years in South Africa (1844–1849) in bold hunting exploits. A rugged outdoorsman with a full red beard, he was a crack shot, widely celebrated in the bush and in London, where he later displayed his trophies and related his escapades to paying crowds. Here he describes a horseback chase of "ten colossal giraffes."

*The sensations which I felt on this occasion were different from any thing that I had before experienced during a long sporting career. My senses were so absorbed by the wondrous and beautiful sight before me that I rode along like one entranced, and felt inclined to disbelieve that I was hunting living things of this world. The ground was firm and favorable for riding. At every stride I gained upon the giraffes, and after a short burst at a swinging gallop I was in the middle*

*of them, and turned the finest cow out of the herd. On finding
herself driven from her comrades and hotly pursued, she increased
her pace, and cantered along with tremendous strides. . . . In a
few minutes I was riding within five yards of her stern, and, firing at the gallop, I sent a bullet into her back. Increasing my
pace, I next rode alongside, and, placing the muzzle of my rifle
within a few feet of her, I fired my second shot behind the shoulder; the ball, however, seemed to have little effect. I then placed
myself directly in front, when she came to a walk. Dismounting,
I hastily loaded both barrels, putting in double charges of powder.
Before this was accomplished she was off at a canter. In a short
time I brought her to a stand in the dry bed of a watercourse,
where I fired at fifteen yards, aiming where I thought the heart
lay, upon which she again made off. Having loaded, I followed,
and had very nearly lost her; she had turned abruptly to the left,
and was far out of sight among the trees. Once more I brought
her to a stand, and dismounted from my horse. There we stood
together alone in the wild wood. I gazed in wonder at her
extreme beauty, while her soft dark eye, with its silky fringe,
looked down imploringly at me, and I really felt a pang of sorrow
in this moment of triumph for the blood I was shedding. Pointing my rifle toward the skies, I sent a bullet through her neck.
On receiving it, she reared high on her hind legs, and fell backward with a heavy crash, making the earth shake around her.
A thick stream of dark blood spouted out from the wound, her
colossal limbs quivered for a moment, and she expired. . . .*
—Roualeyn Gordon Cumming, 1850

Gordon Cumming's remorse did not slow him down.
Thirty pages later he kills another, a "magnificent specimen"
more than eighteen feet tall.

Most of the shooters assured readers of the grave dangers
they faced, but these turned out to be such questionable haz-
ards as torn clothing, nasty thorn scratches, and rough footing. Frederick C. Selous, who read Gordon Cumming at the
age of thirteen and later enjoyed a reputation as the greatest
White Hunter of them all, suffered more serious injuries: he
cracked his tibia and lost a front tooth when his horse galloped
into an anteater hole and he fell upon his own rifle. For
Selous, that only heightened the mystique.

*I never hurt myself seriously, and the risk of such little mis-adventures when galloping after giraffes through thick forests and over ground where the holes were hidden by long grass always added zest to the pursuit of these animals.*
—Frederick C. Selous, 1908

In 1909 Selous led Theodore Roosevelt and his son Kermit on safari through East Africa, a nearly year-long event that amassed more than five hundred animal trophies for the Smithsonian, the American Museum of Natural History, and TR's own considerable pleasure. He shot at least half a dozen giraffes on his own. At one point, while stalking reticulated giraffes in northern Kenya, the former president approached a large female who seemed to be napping, her head tucked among the branches of an acacia tree. When he got just ten feet away, the giraffe opened her eyes and reared up, lashing out at him with her front left hoof. The lethal chop missed the dauntless TR, and as he and his safari-mates laughed heartily, she casually strolled off.

For a number of hunters, that's about as dicey as it got.

*The pleasure of a giraffe hunt is indisputable, but it is one that no real sportsman will repeat more than twice. . . . The trouble is that beyond the chance of being thrown or of coming in contact with a tree, there is not much danger in the pursuit of the giraffe. No animal could be more gentle or defenceless. You have the thrilling excitement of a twenty minutes' burst, but you miss what should be the spice of big-game hunting—the risk. All that you need in giraffe-hunting is a good nag. . . .*
—Harper's Weekly, 1897

*Certainly one can scarcely consider it an elevating form of sport—too often it is lowering for the giraffe, as well as for horse and ride—for it calls forth neither endurance, courage, nor extraordinary skill on the part of the hunter. Practically speaking, if he has a good horse which he can stick to, and can hit a haystack, there is not the slightest reason why he should not count his slain giraffe by the score.*
—Frederick Vaughan Kirby, British hunter, 1896

*For some unaccountable reason, the giraffe is a favorite of trophy hunters. Its head, stuffed with papier-mâché and a pair of glassy, expressionless eyes, decorates many a sportsman's den—and I use the word "sportsman" loosely, since walking up to a giraffe in the field and dropping it in its tracks must involve all the excitement and danger of bagging a Jersey heifer in a dairy yard.*
            —Ken Stott Jr., San Diego Zoo general curator, 1953

So why bother if it wasn't sporting? Well, there was science. And there was meat—a feast for a village, but only the cows. The old bulls were considered inedible, so foul smelling that the Boers called them "stink-bulls."

Then there is the money. Six hundred years ago Albertus Magnus noted that "Giraffe pelts are sold at high prices because of their elegant fur." That was only part of the commercial appeal. The inch-thick hide, tougher and lighter than that of other animals, has been used for boots, drums, buckets, and shields and was the only source of an unbroken strip of leather to fashion the thirty-foot-long whips called *sjamboks* used by the Boers. The rest of the giraffe was equally versatile. Leg tendons became thread and guitar strings; the bones, buttons; the bladder, a water bag. But the prize was the tail. Bracelets were made of the long hairs at the end, or the entire tuft was used as a flyswatter, a coveted symbol of authority that dates back to ancient Egypt. In 1931 the skins of so many giraffes killed along the Kenya railway were turning up minus their tails, the Kenya government was forced to issue a stern directive to its staff:

*In future the guard of a train which has run down and killed a giraffe must, if at all possible, cut the tail off and take it to the nearest station or despatch to the Game Warden, Nairobi. Station Master will give guard a receipt for the tail, and book it on a free parcels waybill to Game Warden, Nairobi, by first passenger train. The hide of the animal should also be sent to the Game Warden, Nairobi, as soon as possible.*
            —Kenya government notice, 1931

It wasn't just trains. In 1928, according to one visitor, the revenue from a giraffe tail would pay an African's house tax for three years.

Kill a giraffe for its tail? For decoration?

*Why? What kind of person can shoot a girafffe? It can't be for sport, because giraffe just stand there and look at you through those long eyelashes. How could anyone pull the trigger? For a rug?*
                    *—Betty Leslie-Melville, giraffe raiser, 1977*

Carl Akeley was a gifted naturalist whose taxidermic method of mounting animals in their natural habitat led to the Akeley African Hall, still the centerpiece of New York's American Museum of Natural History. All three giraffes currently gathered at the waterhole there were shot by Akeley and a colleague. His wife, Mary, an accomplished scientist who shared his objective, nonetheless found the process unbearably sad.

*At last my husband's painstaking efforts were rewarded. The big bull, now at close range, appeared colossal in contrast with the young bulls and females. He actually stood for us. Two shots, a short run of five hundred yards, and the old monarch's reign was finished forever.*

*The rest of the herd stampeded for a short distance only, and then traveled slowly away, stopping frequently to look back for their missing chief. Distress,*

Hand-colored engraving, London, 1813. The description points out that this much-hunted animal "is mild and inoffensive, taking to flight in all cases of danger."

*dejection, amazement that this thing could have happened, were all depicted in their movements as they reluctantly left the spot where their leader had fallen. I doubt not but that they came again and again at nightfall to look for him.*
                    *—Mary Jobe Akeley, 1929*

A number of hunters were similarly swayed, believing that the consequence of their sport made it wrong to continue. Their conversion, generally in the wake of a bloody rout, came too late for the hundreds, perhaps thousands, that had already been eliminated. Sir Samuel Baker, the Nile explorer, underwent his radical about-face in the field. After shooting two in East Africa in 1861, he boasted, "These were my first giraffes, and I admired them as they lay before me with a hunter's pride and satisfaction, but mingled with a feeling of pity for such beautiful and utterly helpless creatures." Years later he was totally transformed.

> *I have never taken any great pleasure in shooting giraffes, as they have always appeared to me the most harmless creatures that exist. They never invade the natives' crops, neither do they attack any animals, or man, but they simply enjoy themselves in their harmless manner. . . .*
> *I have never pursued them except upon occasions when my people were devoid of meat, as the destruction of such lovely creatures without some necessary purpose I regarded as wanton cruelty.*
> *—Sir Samuel Baker, 1890*

> *Moreover, they are such strangely beautiful, such grotesquely graceful creatures, and withal so harmless, that one feels some hesitation in slaying them except for urgent needs. It is a particularly lovely sight to see from an eminence or opposing slope the lofty necks of a herd towering above a sea of bush, with the early morning sun full upon them, standing out conspicuously under its brightening rays against the background of dark green.*
> *—Arthur H. Neumann, elephant hunter, 1899*

> *I cannot describe the impression that I had in seeing one of these gigantic beasts fall, but, frankly, it was with a great deal of regret that I witnessed it. I have no desire to shoot another giraffe. It looked so helpless, and tumbled over as if a church steeple was falling.*
> *—Percy C. Madeira, American hunter, 1909*

*How can one look unmoved at this great noble creature, practically devoid of weapons of defence, when, hopeless of escape, he slackens speed and turns round to face you squarely, without shrinking, without sound, without attempt at revenge, whilst the great teardrops course one another down its face, welling from soft, dark, languishing eyes that have not their equal for beauty upon earth? Can you look on your handiwork without a feeling of deepest pity, fatal to all pleasure, and of regret that the first cruel shot has ever been fired? Merely the freak of a fanciful mind, is it? I should be loth to think so, even though you who do will take keener delight in giraffe-hunting than I. . . . [S]urely then the tearful eyes, the twitching mouth, the quivering limbs of the helpless giraffe, as it stands with reddened sides—gazing down, one can imagine, half scornfully, half beseechingly—express wonder at man's inhumanity besides its own bitter pain!*
*—Frederick V. Kirby, 1896*

Kirby, onetime correspondent for a sportsmen's publication, so regretted killing an old bull giraffe in South Africa, he dramatically considered smashing his rifle to fragments if it would have revived the fallen quarry. Then he got real.

*But why should I try to excuse myself? Why do deliberate, premeditated harm first, and then wish it undone? No, excuses avail nothing—at least do not offer them as excuses—it is unmanly.*

There it is again—that thing about manliness. Few Americans in public life have brandished it as bluntly as President Theodore Roosevelt, the intrepid Rough Rider whose passion for the hunt was matched by an equal commitment to preservation. In 1903 he traveled to Yosemite, California, for a camping trip with John Muir, the ardent conservationist and devoted wildlife authority who had never slain an animal in his life. One night over the campfire, Muir quietly made his point. "Mr. Roosevelt," he asked, "when are you going to get beyond the boyishness of killing things?"

# CHAPTER SEVEN

# Famous Giraffes in History

**A**lthough giraffes tend to run in herds, a number of individuals have distinguished themselves over the centuries. Not that they asked for their fifteen minutes. Their fame was involuntary, a consequence of human design —particularly those Middle Eastern rulers who early discovered the value of a large spotted animal as an instrument of foreign policy. A London newspaper took a cynical view:

> *Despots are the best collectors; and from the fall of the Roman Empire till the arrival of those placed in the Zoological Gardens in 1836, the rare appearances of the giraffe in Europe were in each case due to the munificence of Eastern Sultans and Pashas.*
> —London Spectator, *1892*

We begin more than five hundred years ago:

## The Renaissance Giraffe

Lorenzo de' Medici hadn't asked for a giraffe. He didn't have to. The eminent Florentine statesman, poet, and patron of the arts was widely respected for his superb private collection of imported animals—the best in all of Italy. So when the sultan of Egypt wanted to fortify his ties with Florence (and perhaps cement a recent trade pact), he sent one along in November 1487. By all accounts, the eleven-foot-tall, sienna-skinned beauty with its rays of white lines was a real crowd pleaser —"*molto grande e molto bella e piacevola*" (very tall, very beautiful, and pleasing), in the words of Florentine diarist Luca Landucci. For several years the sweet-tempered visitor entranced the citizens of Florence, nibbling fruit from the hands of young girls and poking its head into second-story windows for apples during daily walks through the city. One historian pronounced it "the most popular character in Florence." Back at Lorenzo's zoo, where the giraffe easily outran the Medici horses, poet Antonio Costanzo took particular notice of the animal's unusual method of walking and, in a letter to a friend, described its "proud gait and full majesty." The giraffe "rises and falls one one side, then the other," he wrote. And it was so affable: "Ours appears to like the crowd, it is always peaceable and without fear, it even seems to watch with pleasure the people who come to look at it." Costanzo also composed a poem from the giraffe to Lorenzo, chiding Pliny, Strabo, and other ancient authors for neglecting to mention its horns!

In a book for young adults, the author fictionalized the town's reaction through the eyes of a teenager named Guido:

> *Peering around a guard, Guido at last saw the giraffe herself. His heart gave a great leap as he gazed at the huge unbelievable creature. She was lying down, her front and hind legs folded alongside of her like the cows. Her large ears were cowlike too. But there the resemblance ended, for she was like no other animal he had ever seen or imagined. Her body, and incredibly long neck edged with a short brush-like mane, looked as if a cream-colored net with large meshes had been thrown over a russet hide. She appeared to be a proud, aloof animal, carrying her head with its two*

*astonishing skin-covered horns daintily aloft. She was chew-*
*ing her cud thoughtfully.*

*The giraffe turned her head just them, and looked at*
*Guido with a gentle expression in her large brown eyes with*
*their long dark lashes. A flood of happiness filled him. . . .*
*She was such a fascinating animal that he could have*
*watched her for hours.*
        —*Willoughby Patton,* The Florentine Giraffe, *1967*

Lorenzo's giraffe became a favorite subject for jewelers, balladeers, and artists of every medium.  Piero di Cosimo included the gentle creature in the right-hand corner of his allegorical painting *Aeolus, as Teacher of Mankind.* Andrea del Sarto's fresco *The Tribute Present to Julius Caeser in Egypt* contains a giraffe in the background. Giorgio Vasari re-created the actual gift-giving ceremony in a fresco at the Palazzo Vecchio entitled *Lorenzo de' Medici Receiving the Ambassadors.* In his zeal, he inexplicably included two extra giraffes in the scene.

**Presentation of the giraffe to Lorenzo de' Medici, as visualized by Vasari. Note the animal's two companions, courtesy of the artist.**

Ironically, the beast that fascinated Florence is today immortalized by one of its old rivals, the nearby town of Siena, where one of the con-trade, or wards, is called the *Contrada della giraffa.* Its motto: "The higher the head, the greater the glory."

Word of the Florentine giraffe also reached France, where Anne of Beaujeu, regent of France (she was the eldest daughter of Louis XI and had inherited his menagerie), longed to enlarge her own collection. In a letter to Lorenzo dated April 15, 1489, she wrote:

*You know that formerly you advised me in writing that you would send me the giraffe, and although I am sure that you will keep your promise, I beg you, nevertheless, to deliver the animal to me and send it this way, so that you may understand the affection I have for it; for this is the beast of the world that I have the greatest desire to see. And if there is any thing on this side I can do for you, I shall apply myself to it with all my heart.*

History does not record whether Lorenzo had in fact made such a promise or whether Anne's competitive spirit was at work; in any event, she did not get her wish. The beast was already dead, and France would have to wait another three centuries for its own giraffe.

## The Giraffe Who Walked to Paris

The year was 1826; the scene, Alexandria, Egypt. Persuaded by the French consul general that Franco-Egyptian relations might benefit if King Charles X received the first living giraffe in his country (and the first in Western Europe since Lorenzo's), Mohammed Ali, the viceroy and pasha of Egypt, readily agreed and dispatched his soldiers to Sudan to capture an appropriate candidate. There was ample precedent. Other African sovereigns had curried favor with the court at Versailles by presenting gifts of lions, panthers, and gazelles.

Luckily the new hunt yielded two baby giraffes, because when word of the French consul's coup leaked out, the English consul requested a keepsake for his king, too. How to decide which creature—one taller and sturdier than the other—would go where? The pasha's judgment was Solomonic: the diplomats would draw lots for the animals. "I am happy to inform Your Excellency that the drawing was favorable to us," reported the Frenchman in a triumphant dispatch. "Our giraffe is strong and vigorous, the one given to the king of England is sickly and will not live long." His smug observation was a sadly accurate prophesy (see page 110).

But the healthy giraffe was destined to embark on an unprecedented journey, to a land where almost no one had ever seen anything like her. What they did know came from second-hand reports. Ecstatic over their impending good fortune—mindful that it was a precious gift for their king—scientists at Paris' Natural History Museum insisted on every precaution for the health and care of their exotic guest. She was, to put it mildly, pampered.

A two-masted sailing ship was engaged to transport her from Alexandria, with a hole specially cut in the deck so the giraffe could stand in the hold and poke her head into the sea air. A tarpaulin was rigged over the opening to protect her from harsh weather, and the entire area was

*Study of the Giraffe Given to Charles X* by Nicolas Hûet

padded with straw to cushion her against the waves. Thus ensconced, she set off in October 1826, accompanied by her accomplished keeper, Hassan; two young Sudanese companions, named Atir and Yussef, to keep her from being lonely; and three cows to provide her daily ration of milk. Around her neck she wore a strip of parchment inscribed with verses from the Koran for further safekeeping. Almost two years old and just over eleven feet tall, she was about to conquer France.

October 23, 1826: With its only casualty a seasick cow, the giraffe-bearing brigantine sailed into Marseilles. The regal passenger had tolerated her two-week trip splendidly and, after an unavoidable bureaucratic delay of three more weeks in quarantine, was finally led onto French soil. Officials scheduled the grand entrance for 10 P.M. to avoid the crowds and jubilantly led her to her new temporary home: a specially built pen right next door to the town prefect. She would spend the winter in Marseilles and adjust to the European climate.

It would be impossible to exaggerate the impact of this *belle enfant des tropiques*. In Marseilles she was a grand celebrity, dressed in a special body cloth decorated with the arms of France. She was the subject of a daily column in the newspaper; she was the coveted star of numerous dinner parties given by the prefect's wife, during which honored guests in evening clothes would troop off to her stable to observe her by torchlight. Regular folks could see her during her daily promenade, a 12–2 P.M. event that drew hordes. A French novelist captured the mood in a fictional version of the occasion:

> *The people of Marseilles flocked to the gates of City Hall to see the stupendous beast—and the Negro herdsmen. The prefect's popularity soared. Each day the ceremony proceeded in the same orderly fashion: the clock struck noon, the main gate opened, the gendarmes fell into two parallel lines, and the giraffe came out, almost in slow motion, with Atir holding a lead on one side, Yussef on the other. . . . A governmental employee trailed the procession deep into the outskirts of town, using a shovel and a strange-looking green broom to collect Her Highness's inevitable droppings. Under orders from the countess, they became fertilizer for her private garden. Around two o'clock, the little troupe would reenter the City Hall grounds, to the applause of the last onlookers. The gardener would take delivery of the wheelbarrow full of still-steaming dung and proudly deposit it at the foot of the rosebushes.*
> —Marie Nimier, The Giraffe, *1995*

From Paris, eager scientists demanded a long list of statistics. Under their instructions, the giraffe was measured (eleven feet three inches), watched, tended, adored, and sketched— just in case she expired before they met her. While they waited, they worried and plotted. How to complete her journey and deliver her to them, and to the king? Finally it was decided: the giraffe would walk to Paris. It would take more than a month to cover the five hundred or so miles, but she would proceed at a leisurely pace of some fifteen miles a day. That, it was determined, would both safeguard her health and satisfy the curiosity of the public. As an extra nod to popular demand, she would stop each night at a different inn, official giraffe way stations identified by signs decorated with her picture.

To supervise this exquisitely choreographed march, Paris dispatched renowned naturalist and zoology professor Geoffroy Saint-Hilaire. At fifty-five he was a formidable specimen himself, whose own reputation was about to be ensured by this grand responsibility.

On May 20, 1827, the caravan departed, with all the bearings of a royal procession. Up front, two police on horseback stopped traffic. Then came the commander of the local police brigade and three officers who escorted the parade to the border of the next town. They were followed by the milk cows tended by several Egyptians in full Oriental regalia. Geoffroy Saint-Hilaire came next—usually marching in solitary splendor but occasionally inviting a local dignitary to join him in the position of honor. At last came Dame Girafe, her keepers gripping a cord that was attached to her bridle. She was not the least bit bashful, and they allowed her great freedom of movement. Bringing up the rear was a horse-drawn carriage with baggage and several cages containing an antelope and wild sheep sent along as additional gifts.

It was an awesome array, especially when it rained. The giraffe's gracious hosts, concerned about the possibility of pneumonia after a chilly shower, had thoughtfully ordered up a waterproof raincoat, made to measure from gummed canvas. It covered her entire body and buttoned conveniently along the front of her neck, sporting the arms of the pasha on one side and those of the king on the other. Gabriel Dardaud, the French journalist who rediscovered this largely forgotten story during his posting in the Middle East a century after the fact, pronounced the outfit "more practical than aesthetic."

Crowds lined the entire route, and newspapers chronicled her every step. The giraffe, thriving on her diet of twenty to twenty-five liters of milk a day, plus all the leaves she could reach, was cheered and beloved. She stopped at Aix, Lambesc, Orgon, Avignon, and Orange, her progress relayed by the har-

ried Saint-Hilaire to the interior minister from every post
office along the way. He also complained about the inns,
where he encountered bad food, dirty linens, and bedbugs.

The giraffe seemed blissfully at ease. There were only two
untoward incidents—a nail in her hoof, which was removed successfully; and a bit of a romp with some unruly horses in Lyon.
Otherwise, she marched through France in perfect calm, with
the bemused attitude of a seasoned traveler who knows she's a
hit.

At 5 P.M. on June 30, 1827, the giraffe arrived in Paris, her
entrance heralded by masses of Parisians. The novelist Stend-
hal organized a riverboat "giraffe party" on the Seine to watch
her pass. Just over a week later she was brought to the king at
his summer palace at St. Cloud, outside the city. Once again
police lined the route; once again the giraffe wore a coat with
twin coats of arms. And behaved like a perfect lady. She ate
rose petals from the king's hand. She stood calmly while the
duchess of Berry placed a garland of flowers around her neck.
She let the royal children touch her spotted skin. And the king
rewarded her keepers with thousands of francs. She was, in
short, a royal success.

Later that evening the giraffe returned to the Jardin des
Plantes, the lush botanical gardens that had been turned into

**Ticket to see the giraffe**

Paris' first zoo, where she became the most important celebrity in all of France. That year, 1827, became "the year of the giraffe." During the last six months alone, more than six hundred thousand Parisians purchased tickets to see her. VIPs got a closer look for twice the price. Unless there was inclement weather, she was promenaded every afternoon past the quays of the Seine, with visitors straining behind the barricades for the entire two-hour viewing.

In the spring and summer she ate greenery, and in winter, hay and vegetables. Her personal favorite was onions, although just about anything disappeared into her sinuous tongue. To spare her indigestion, keepers finally asked visitors not to bring bouquets.

Paris fairly worshiped the giraffe. She starred in drawings, paintings (a new version every week, sold outside the Jardin des Plantes), woodcuts, music (a waltz for piano, a guitar number, a romance), and poetry. Her image was everywhere: on almanacs, faience plates, shaving bowls, pitchers, wineglasses, irons, matchboxs, toothpicks, bed pillows. There were giraffe toys, giraffe makeup tables, gingerbread giraffes. Women carried handbags with giraffes and stitched petit point screens or pincushions in their image. Everything chic was *à la girafe*—a collar worn by fashionable ladies (made of an amulet like the one the giraffe wore, suspended from a narrow ribbon), colors, hairdos, hats, and scarves. And a

**Plates (and shaving bowl) depicting *la girafe***

particularly bad winter health epidemic was dubbed by the doctors *grippe de la girafe*.

The scientists were in heaven, meticulously noting every detail of her daily life. A philosopher devoted an entire page to an examination of the purpose of the giraffe. The only threat to Her Spotted Majesty's reign over Paris that August was the arrival of some Osage Indians from Oklahoma. Curious Parisians lined up to see them as well, but the giraffe held her own.

Eventually, through no fault of her own, the royal connections that had brought her to France caused her luster to tarnish. Liberals opposed to the unpopular king made her a political pawn; Chateaubriand, one of their leaders, circulated a treatise called *The Giraffe, or the Government of Beasts*. Others subverted the diplomatic mission of the giraffe (to gain support for the pasha, who was backing the Ottoman sultan in putting down a rebellion in Greece) by criticizing the Egyptian ruler.

A caricaturist turned the giraffe into Charles X with the caption "The largest beast one has ever seen." A medal with the image of the giraffe parodied a phrase the king had made famous: "Nothing has changed in France except there is another great beast."

By June of 1830 the phenomenon was *fini*. Few people visited her, fewer still talked about her. She no longer dominated dinner table conversation or ladies' magazines. Balzac used the decline of the giraffe's popularity to predict the imminent downfall of the king. He was right. After riots and revolution later that summer, Louis-Philippe took the throne and Charles X went into exile.

The giraffe remained but was largely forgotten. Concerned caretakers sought a mate for their guest, then settled for a female, who provided welcome companionship.

In 1845 the giraffe who walked to Paris died. She was about twenty-one years old. In the interest of science, she was dissected and skinned, then stuffed and placed in the gallery of the Natural History Museum, where the public could visit her every Tuesday and Friday. Eugène Delacroix, the French Romantic painter, stopped in to see her in 1847. He wrote in his journal that the giraffe had become a moral principle, "dying in obscurity as complete as his entry in the world had been brilliant. Here he is, all stiff and clumsy as nature made him."

Delacroix missed both the giraffe's gender and the point. It was man, not nature, that had turned the elegant creature into a clumsy exhibit—but Gallic loyalty almost resurrected her. For years a patriotic rumor circulated that the famous French giraffe had been placed in a museum in Verdun, where the military considered using her in the trenches during World War I to scare German troops. Another story claimed that after ruinous bombing there, her graceful neck was the only thing left amid the rubble of the museum.

Inspiring, but false. The stuffed giraffe was sent to the Natural History Museum in La Rochelle, a west coast town she had bypassed on her famous walk north. There, she was displayed next to the camel on which Napoleon explored the Suez desert during his Egyptian campaign. The camel has moved on, but *la girafe* endures, a relic of diplomacy, a victim

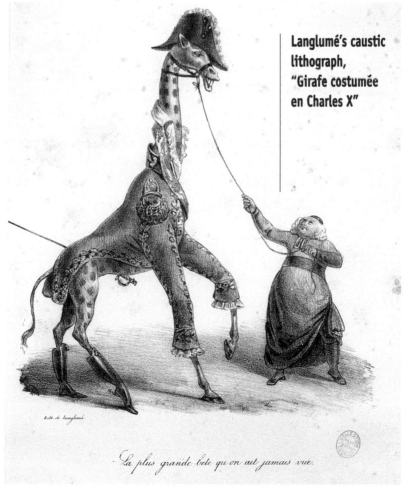

Langlumé's caustic lithograph, "Girafe costumée en Charles X"

*La plus grande bête qu'on ait jamais vue.*

"The Camelopard, or a New Hobby" by satirist William Heath (Paul Pry), 1827

of public whim, a scrawny souvenir of the world's only real royal highness.

## George IV's Giraffe

The smaller, frailer giraffe sent to England in 1827 enjoyed neither the long life nor the goodwill of her French cousin. After a winter in Malta and a sea voyage to England,

**"State of the Giraffe" by William Heath, 1829**

she arrived at Windsor in August 1827, where, according to a contemporary account, "the King himself hastened to inspect his extraordinary acquisition, and was greatly pleased with the care that had been taken to bring it to his presence in fine order."

For George IV, who had a passion for the bizarre, the giraffe was the perfect gift. He had a special pen and paddock built for it on the grounds and commissioned two fine portraits of his new pet. But like his counterpart across the Channel, the king faced widespread political opposition. And for them, the giraffe was simply a huge, irresistible target.

Cartoonists took aim at the king's extravagant tastes and ample girth, saving their most pointed pens for his even more ample companion, Lady Conyngham. One caricature put the chubby pair astride the giraffe. Another portrayed the monarch as a Chinese mandarin fondling his new toy.

All the while, the fragile giraffe—who received few crowds and little adulation—deteriorated. As a British journal noted, "Its legs almost lost their power of supporting the body, the joints seemed to shoot over; and at length the weakness increased to such a degree that it became necessary to have a pulley constructed, which, being suspended from the ceiling of the animal's hovel, was fastened round its body, for the purpose of raising it on its legs without any exertion on its own part." In the humiliation, not to mention obvious discomfort, of this makeshift sling, the poor beast suffered for months. Once again the cartoonists exulted. Paul Pry (the pen name of William Heath) drew a wicked picture of the king and Lady Conyngham winching the giraffe upright, with a comment in the margin reflecting antagonism toward the monarch and his lavish ways: "I suppose we shall have to pay for stuffing him next."

Right on the mark. After two years and two months at Windsor, the giraffe died at the age of four on October 11, 1829. Poor King George. His father had lost the colonies, and he couldn't even hold on to a giraffe. Yet another satiric lithograph marked the occasion. This one, encased in a funereal black border, showed the royal twosome weeping over the prostrate corpse. Which was, of course, skinned, stuffed, and preserved at the Zoological Society. Its current fate is unknown, but a century and a half did quite a lot to change the British attitude toward their giraffes, as the story of Victor (see page 118) explains.

## Daisy Rothschild

We turn now to the story of a contemporary enchantress, a giant from Kenya whose legacy continues to charm thousands of modern-day visitors. The woman who made her famous described their first meeting:

*"It's a girl!" The phrase jerked me suddenly back to twenty-three years earlier, when my daughter was born. Little was I to know that the next time I would have a personal interest in the news would be about a beautiful brown-eyed, eight-foot-tall, 450-pound baby giraffe.*

*There she lay, uncomfortable and undignified in the short marshy grass, with one rear foot tied to the opposite front foot by a rope, and Kiborr straddled across her, struggling to hold her long neck upright. . . .*

*For us it was love at first sight—we adored her instantly. She hated us.*

*Her enormous brown eyes glared at us in fright, and those long long eyelashes made her look like a very angry daisy indeed. We touched her; she was so soft—not coarse at all, but silky like a puppy. I kissed her nose. I kissed her on her head and patted her. Her little horns were tufted; they looked like two black paintbrushes sticking up out of her head. Her mane was a golden brown and shaped as perfectly as if it had been cut by Sassoon. Three brown butterfly-shaped spots ran down her beige neck in a row. Beautiful.*

*—Betty Leslie-Melville, 1977*

**Daisy Rothschild (right) and Betty Leslie-Melville at Giraffe Manor**

The besotted writer is an American named Betty Leslie-
Melville who, with her late husband, Jock, decided to adopt a
baby Rothschild giraffe to raise on the grounds of their fifteen-
acre property in the suburbs of Nairobi. They were inspired
by the impending development of the giraffe's land on a cattle
ranch in Soy and wanted to be sure the 130 members of the
herd there were not doomed to extinction. So in 1974 they
arranged for a capture and brought the unwitting creature
home. They named her Daisy Rothschild.

Thus began a wonderful adventure, with both the Leslie-
Melvilles and their unlikely lodger learning more about each
other than either thought possible. Betty and Jock bonded with
Daisy; they fed her by hand, suffering bites from baby giraffe
teeth and worrying over unimagined sicknesses, over leaving
her alone, over such unanticipated booby traps as clotheslines

**Daisy et al., Giraffe Manor.**

and barbed wire. Under their patient and loving care, she
thrived, a gentle and loyal and always entertaining member of
the household. Determined she would not be a pet, the Leslie-
Melvilles set her free and were ecstatic when she returned to
share at least part of her life with her human family.

In time they worried about Daisy's future and decided to
obtain a companion for her. Once again they hired a hunter;
once again they fell in love, this time with a young male.

*As the day wore on he couldn't resist looking at us more
often, and soon he came up and gently put his face next to
mine and let me touch him for the first time. Just when he
saw how I melted and how much I was enjoying caressing
his soft downy nose, he lunged again at the opening, almost
knocking me down in his effort to get out. He kept repeating*

*the same procedure, getting us to lower our guard by being*
*sweet and then making another attempt at jailbreaking.*
    *What an actor! And so beautiful! We named him*
*Marlon. As in Brando.*
                        *—Betty Leslie-Melville, 1977*

I met Marlon and Daisy in 1985, when, like many visitors before and since, I had the great pleasure of staying at their renamed home, Giraffe Manor. Every morning I woke up to the sight of them and the rest of the gorgeous gang: Betty June; her mate, Gilman; their daughter, Buttercup; and the always macho John Paul. At breakfast they reached through the open windows and shared our cereal. Later, at their feeding station, they presented their huge heads for handouts and caresses. It was an unearthly experience, and I found myself wondering how anyone could live without giraffes on the front lawn.

Daisy's stardom spread to the States. Betty and Jock wrote her biography (*Raising Daisy Rothschild*) and TV made a movie (*The Last Giraffe*), although the role of Daisy was played by another animal. Even aging giraffes need a stand-in for close-ups.

In 1989 Daisy died, but the herd she left behind continues to flourish. The Rothschild population in Kenya has stabilized at about five hundred, largely because many have been translocated to parks where they have room to roam. Today Betty's son and daughter-in-law, Bryony and Rick Anderson, run Giraffe Manor, where you can visit and stay and meet the current Rothschilds-in-residence, including Baby Daisy (a namesake, not a descendant), Buttercup, Jock (in honor of his late human forebear), and Jock's offspring: Uhuru, Arlene, Laura, and Butterfly, who was a reticent four-month-old calf when I last visited at Christmas, 1996. Perhaps by the time you get there, she will have grown as bold as her kinfolk, readily offering a satiny nose and a fluid tongue to a kindly caller bearing food pellets. I confess to indulging the giraffes during my recent sojourn. Or perhaps I just indulged myself. Could you say no to an eyelash-batting beggar poking her head through the breakfast-room window?

While there I learned that some 90,000 visitors have come to Giraffe Manor, now an educational center operated by the African Fund for Endangered Wildlife. Schoolchildren are a spe-

**Giraffes also have very sweet breath.**

cial priority, especially African school children, since the center claims that 85 percent of Africans have never seen wild animals.

In summarizing the intent of their grand venture, Betty Leslie-Melville wrote, "How terrible if future generations have to ask, 'What was a giraffe?'" Just in case, she's left these reminders:

*Marlon has even taken to doing impersonations. Sometimes he looks like an ostrich, and sometimes he looks like a duck. He can also look like a deer, a chipmunk, and even an airplane, and always he feels like a pussy willow. They're both irresistible and seem so like people to me at times that I wonder why they don't have arms.*

*They make our hearts sing. . . .*

*I keep searching for a flaw—it isn't fair to be without blemish. . . .*

*In fact, sometimes it all seems too perfect—like Never Never Land, or a Rousseau painting come to life. There are even moments when we wonder if we have died and gone to heaven. No one in Sunday school told me that heaven is filled with giraffe; if they had I might have paid more attention.*

*—Betty Leslie-Melville, 1977*

## Victor, Victoria

And then there is Victor. For pure pathos, nothing beats the tender story of the hapless giraffe from the zoo in England who gave his life for the cow he loved.

Victor was fifteen years old, a sturdy eighteen-footer at Marwell Park Zoo near Winchester, seventy miles southwest of London. He was also the only bull in the shop, so zookeepers eagerly endorsed his romantic intentions with the three females next door. It was not their first date. But fate was not kind that Thursday evening in September 1977. Something apparently happened when Victor mounted his mate: either she stepped forward, or he slipped, or perhaps the earth just moved. Whatever the cause, Victor lay spread-eagle on the ground—a perilous position for any giraffe, let alone one caught up in the passion of the moment. When a giraffe does the splits, as it's known, a ton or more of weight lands on four relatively spindly legs, damaging the muscles as they collapse into a position never intended by nature. Victor, his hind legs splayed on either side of his massive body, was in terrible trouble.

**Victor, helpless**

The first rescuers called to the scene were the local fire brigade, who, after four hours of unsuccessful pushing and prodding, slipped air bags underneath the fallen lover and inflated them, as if he were any other damaged conveyance. That raised the giraffe a foot and a half, to his knees, but led to no further activity.

Victor wouldn't, or couldn't, budge.

Next morning the zoo's manager reported no progress but added, "He is in a reasonable frame of mind. If we just let him have a bit of peace and quiet, it is our hope that in time, he will revive some interest in himself and get up."

Anxious keepers thought a little flirtation might help and paraded his three erstwhile paramours—Arabesque, Domino, and Dribbles— before him. Victor failed to rise to the occasion.

Meanwhile he was weakening. Vets tried to boost his energy with immense doses of vitamins and with glucose from an intravenous drip suspended above his still perpendicular neck. They also injected him with penicillin. Sympathetic crowds who had gathered around his pen cheered when he nibbled at some freshly cut grass. But when his neck started to droop, his personal caretaker, twenty-one-year-old Ruth Giles, supported his head and sobbed.

Eyewitnesses swear that from time to time a tear rolled silently down Victor's elegant, spotted cheek.

Victor and helpers (top); Victor and Ruth Giles (middle); Victor toughs it out (bottom)

By Sunday the story of the gentle giant's accident was dominating headlines around the world, leading to stacks of "get well" telegrams and hundreds of messages of help. The Royal Air Force and Navy volunteered lifting gear and a helicopter. Haulage men offered cranes and earth movers. Both

**The scaffolding rises**

were gratefully declined for fear of crushing Victor's ribs and legs. The Oklahoma City Zoo cabled advice from its own similar experience. An American hypnotist offered his services. Someone suggested digging a swimming pool around Victor to float him to his feet. Zookeepers considered everything as they stacked bales of straw around their patient and covered him with a tarpaulin at night to guard against the chill.

On Monday officials called in the navy. Construction workers started building a steel scaffolding around the toppled giraffe as Her Majesty's sailmakers sewed up a pair of canvas "trousers." They planned to use the garment (really more of a harness) to support his legs while a block and tackle attached to the tower lifted him up. Victor watched in stoic silence as the twenty-five-foot frame took shape around him, blissfully composed as the construction tools clanged and electric drills whirred just inches from his very sensitive ears. "He has taken it all marvelously," Ruth Giles said bravely. "I am trying to keep him as calm as I can." A British newspaper headline reflected public sentiment: HANG ON, VICTOR! It was a far cry from the ridicule heaped on England's first sickly giraffe a century and a half earlier.

On Wednesday the rescue operation was ready. Zoo workers spent two hours lacing Victor into the canvas support, then cranked him up cautiously. Slowly, gingerly, Victor began to rise, all eighteen feet of him vertical for the first time in six days. The ailing beast moved each leg in turn—including the painful rear limb that had been pinned beneath him. His human helpers reached out their arms, desperate to massage the circulation back into action. The operation seemed to be working, and the giraffe, his legs now dangling from the makeshift machine, was being lowered to the ground. Success seemed so near! Then, suddenly, it was over. Quietly, without warning, Victor stopped breathing. His head was cradled by his keeper and his heart ceased to beat. The doctor injected a heart stimulant, but the trauma had been too great. The magnificent creature was dead.

For Ruth Giles, who had barely left his side during the 125-hour ordeal, hand-feeding her charge, calming him with tender words and constantly stroking his elegant skin, the loss was anguishing. For more than two hundred visitors who had kept a vigil at his pen, it was a terrible, tearful shock, and they silently drifted away from the scene. For the millions more at home who had been captivated by Victor's quiet dignity and kept abreast of his progress with hourly news bulletins, it was heartbreaking. Radio stations across Britain interrupted programming with the news flash of his demise. And the normally cynical reporters who had kept Victor's story alive grieved more than the loss of great copy. Beneath a headline reading FAREWELL, DEAR FRIEND, Jean Rook of the *London Daily Express* eulogized the nation's newest martyr:

*He towered 18 ft. above our troubles. He rose above North-ern Ireland, Rhodesia, a breadstrike, and the deaths of Marc Bolan and Maria Callas.*

*He blocked telephone lines, jammed the postal system, and called out the Navy. The very earth shook when he fell.*

*For six anxious days, our thoughts, our news bulletins, and our prayers have been weighed down by a one ton, 15-year-old giraffe. Advice, and tears, have poured into his sick-pen from a nation united, all eyes on the skyline, in their grief.*

*Winch him, float him, excavate him, do any damned thing, at any cost, but get him to his feet, cried strong men in their anguish.*

*"But why can't he just get UP, mum," literally wept children, in their innocence.*

*And every night, and morning, the bulletins were put out on TV and in newspapers. He's rallying. He's sinking. He has a 50-50 chance. We hunched round the reports, breathlessly waiting, like those British who remember the world-famous bulletin on George V: "The King's life is drawing peacefully to its close."*

*Before The Fall, he was just another giraffe. One of those wobbly-legged fur jigsaw puzzles you chuckle at at the zoo.*

*After The Fall, he became a nation's hero. . . . Because the whole country, God bless us, rose to him. And to the grandeur of his fight for life.*

*Who but the British could down tears . . . for a giraffe? Who but this nation of shopkeepers, cat-lovers and dog-walkers, could forget their own social and economic fears, hoping for a miracle for Victor?*

*In Russia, he would have been shot the moment he slipped, as unproductive. In America, they would have banned the too meaningful showing of his violent animal love, and possibly traumatic death, on TV. In the rest of Europe, they'd have shrugged and sent for the dust cart.*

*Only the British could close ranks, shoulder to shoulder, and cheek-to-wet-cheek, to battle, with an almost World War Two sense of comradeship, for the life of a giraffe.*

—*Jean Rook*, London Daily Express, *1977*

Victor was not forgotten. Donations sent in his honor were used to fund a variety of conservation projects. A twelve-foot-tall, two-year-old replacement stud named Pedro Giles (for keeper Ruth Giles) joined the zoo a month later. And across the ocean in Washington, D.C., the story of the lovesick giraffe became an inspiration. A group of admirers formed the Society of Victor Invictus, dedicated to the hardy spirit of the fallen lover. Their symbol: a stylized image of Victor ahoist in his harness. For ten years, under the leadership of co-founder Donal McLaughlin, several hundred fans celebrated Victor's gallantry and memorialized his legacy at annual gatherings— a cruise, a dance, a Valentine's Day love-in. One of the society's members pointed out that age was a factor in their establishment. "Everyone has that terror of growing old, of going downhill," he told *The Washington Post.* "But to die trying— what more can you ask?"

In June 1978 the society and others touched by Victor's plight rejoiced when Dribbles, one of Victor's widows, delivered a bouncing, six-foot-tall baby. Victor, it turns out, had scored—some months before the Fall—and his spirit passed on to his daughter. She was, of course, named Victoria.

# CHAPTER EIGHT

# Tall Tales

Because of its height, the giraffe has long been a symbol of people who just don't fit in: they may be too tall, or too eccentric, or simply too different from everyone else. And that's only one of the connections often made with them. Inexplicably odd and sweetly affable, they've been credited with many mystical powers. I give you my interpretation.

"So, when did you first sense this fear of height?"

© Martin Giuffre. Used with permission.

## The Giraffe as the Gawky Outsider

In the movie *Northwest Mounted Police*, Gary Cooper plays a Texas Ranger who travels to Canada to find a fugitive. As he saunters into the Mounties' barracks—a stranger on alien turf—the lanky American bumps his head on an overhanging lamp. "This place wasn't built for a giraffe," quips one of the Royal Canadians. A round of laughter follows at the tall Texan's expense.

A more imaginative version of the same image seemed perfectly reasonable to a reader of *Parade*:

> *Q. I don't know if it's true, but I've been told that a high official of the Reagan Administration was kidnapped as a baby and raised by a colony of domestic giraffes in Africa. If true, please identify him.*
> *—V. J., Oakland, Calif.*

> *A. The official is David Gergen, a former speechwriter for Richard Nixon who is now assistant to the President for communications. Gergen, however, was never raised by giraffes in Africa; he was reared by humans in Durham, N.C., where he grew to be 6-feet-6. It is because of his height and lope that Howell Raines of "The New York Times" described him in a 1981 article as a man who looks as if he might have been kidnapped in his youth by kindly giraffes who reared him to adulthood.*
> *—Walter C. Scott, Parade, 1983*

At six feet six, Charles de Gaulle was an obvious candidate for giraffe metaphors, a man who so believed in the power of the tall man that he once told John Kenneth Galbraith, "It is important that we be merciless with those who are too small." A short story set in Paris during the Algerian crisis of the late 1950s illustrates how out of step he was perceived to be by those who opposed his support for Algerian independence. This scene takes place as General de Gaulle is being driven into the courtyard of the Élysée Palace:

> *"Into the zoo with the giraffe," the chauffeur said.   He looked into the mirror but could detect no emotion on the*

*General's face. A stupid word, thought the General, it cannot possibly come from the clever little Jew. The little Jew would know what would happen if they started locking giraffes into the zoo. If they locked up tall old generals they would also lock up clever little Jews and soon anybody who did not fit in with the time would be locked up. Into this time, the General thought with contempt, and finally stepped out of the car. He really has something of the giraffe, thought the driver admiringly, watching his general reach the top of the stairs and lean down to the President of the Republic, who had already been waiting up there for some time.*

*—Alfred Andresch,*
*"The Night of the Giraffe," 1964*

Later, the general reflects on his image:

*Before he fell asleep in his bed at Colombey-les-Deux Églises the tall old General thought once more of the gate at the Élysée Palace, the gate reserved for heads of states only, which he had ordered opened because he believed in the power of ceremony, in the magic of rites, in the mesmerism of pantomime. Before the masses he would stretch his long arms above his head in a great, solemn, slow gesture that made him seem even taller than he was. Let them call me giraffe, he thought, the animal that stands high above the veldt.*

Inanimate objects have also been singled out for giraffe treatment. There is a giraffe unicycle, a giraffe radar, and a giraffe harpsichord, all named for their irregular size.

A number of children's books also use this theme to lessen the agony of the youngster who grows faster and taller than society can handle. Children's literature uses giraffes the way it uses all animals—as fables that are "racially and ethnically neutral (and therefore universally acceptable) in a way that human figures cannot be," according to one authority. "They teach us about themselves—and ourselves."

One lesson comes from a giraffe named Raffie, who covets the zebra's stripes and the gnu's beard, until he understands that his own spots make him quite magnificent.

A more vulnerable soul is Helga, an adolescent giraffe who hates her height until she pokes her head in a second-story window and captures a burglar in the act. If you were a tall child, perhaps you had a relative like hers:

*So Helga slumped. Then her Aunt Minnie said, "Not only is Helga very tall, but she has bad posture, too."*
—*Marjorie Weinman Sharmat,* Helga High-Up, *1987*

In another book (which I found catalogued in the Library of Congress under self-acceptance, fiction) a female giraffe named Memily is made to feel self-conscious about her size by the other jungle animals. Anyone who got tall before the rest of the kids will understand:

*Week after week, Memily grew, and she became sadder and sadder. She was shy and embarrassed by her height, and whenever any of the other creatures walked by she would turn her head, knowing that they had to look up just to look her in the eye. Memily grew and grew. She began to bow her neck and bend her knees, trying to make herself shorter. Everything she tried was to no avail, for no matter how much she bowed her neck or bent her knees, she was still very tall indeed.*
—*Stephen Cosgrove,* Memily, *1995*

Finally, a meeting with another giraffe convinces her that she is just right for the animal she is. Memily gallops off with her pal to an inspiring coda: "Short is short and tall is tall. You are what you are, and that is all!"

## The Giraffe as a Creature of Fear

One afternoon I went to the Bronx Zoo and headed into the Carter Giraffe Building, where I stood at the rail and stared up blissfully at a handsome fellow named James V (for zoo benefactor James Carter; all Bronx baby boy giraffes are named James). I was joined shortly by a class of second-graders, chattering and oohing and aahing—except for one child who remained at the rear of the group with his eyes staring straight down. His teacher told me that the little boy, about thigh high to me, had just arrived from the Dominican Republic. He had never seen anything as massive as the spotted giant before him. And he was terrified. It took at least fifteen minutes before he would lift his head to steal a look—a very tentative glance. Then his eyes bulged in awe.

They *are* huge. Which may be why these mild-mannered beasts have been mythologized as terrifying monsters. The author of a medieval animal dictionary in Arabic related this very sinister side of the giraffe:

> *A giraffe seen in a dream indicates a financial calamity. Sometimes it signifies a respectable or beautiful woman, or the receipt of strange news to come from the direction from which the animal is seen. There is, however, no good in the news. When a giraffe appears in a dream to enter a country or town, no gain is to be obtained from it, for it augurs a calamity to your property; there is no guaranty for the safety of a friend, a spouse, or a child whom you may want to take through your homestead. A giraffe in a dream may sometimes be interpreted to mean a wife who is not faithful to her husband, because in the shape of its back it differs from the riding-beasts.*
> *—Damiri, author of animal dictionary, 1371*

In his third-century novel *An Ethiopian Romance*, Heliodorus described a sacrifice to King Hydaspes, the victorious ruler of Ethiopia. When the envoys of the Auxomites, ancestors of present-day Ethiopians, arrived to pay tribute, they brought along a giraffe, which, according to the book, "filled the whole assembly with trepidation." Then it incited a riot:

> *At the altar of the Moon stood a pair of bulls, and at that of the Sun a team of four white horses, duly held ready for the sacrifice. The appearance of that alien, unfamiliar, unheard-of monster caused a great commotion among the victims, as though they beheld some spectre. They were filled with terror and broke the halters by which the attendants held them. One of the bulls—which alone, it seems, had caught sight of the wild beast—and two of the horses sped away in headlong flight. Unable to force their way out of the ring of soldiers, who with a wall of close-locked shields formed a circular barrier of heavy-armed men, they dashed about in distraction, careering and wheeling about the middle space, and upsetting everything that came in their way, whether lifeless object or living creature. Mingled cries of two kinds arose as this was happening—some of fright from people towards whom the animals were rushing, and some of pleasure from those who, as the animals dashed at others, were stirred to amusement and laughter by seeing these people knocked down and trampled on.*
> —Heliodorus, Greek novelist, third century

That fear appears to have been passed down to the men who accompanied a British survey expedition to Lake Chad in 1904.

> *There was a superstition among the natives that the slayer of a giraffe would be inflicted with madness, and peculiar forms of ju-ju had to be observed to avert this fate. Gosling [who killed it] was made to take a certain kind of snuff, and the natives rubbed it on the tops of their heads. The tuft on the head of the giraffe and its whiskers had then to be singed, and Gosling was only just in time to rescue the tail from being cut off.*
> —Lt. Boyd Alexander, British explorer, 1907

On the other hand, fear worked in favor of the pure white giraffe that once lived in northern Tanzania. According to legend, it was safe from hunters because "they associate its colouring with the spirit-infested peak of near-by Kilimanjaro."

## The Giraffe as a Fantasy Figure, Defying Logic, Utterly Surreal

The most uninhibited expressions of this most unlikely animal abound in children's books. Shel Silverstein's *A Giraffe and a Half* regales us with giggly rhymes ("If you had a giraffe . . . and he stretched another half . . . you would have a giraffe and a half"), including one about a giraffe who "put his suit in the laundry chute." In *Emily the Giraffe* the frisky protagonist helpfully gets horizontal to become a diving board for her pals, then holds her neck rigidly vertical to serve as the mast for a sailing boat. *Your Pet Giraffe* (from the Far-Fetched Pets series) warns that while you may wash your pet, "No matter how disgustingly dirty he gets, never use spot remover. He needs his spots to hide from enemies." On a slightly more serious note, *The Girl on the Yellow Giraffe* tells the bewitching story of a youngster empowered by her toy giraffe on wheels, a mode of transport that protects her from harm and emboldens her on her visits throughout the city.

A subset of this category offers up a portrait of the artist as a young giraffe. Author Cecilia Casrill Dartez created Jenny Giraffe to teach youngsters about Louisiana culture. Once, when Jenny finds herself marooned in New Orleans' French Quarter, she is frightened that she'll be captured and caged. In a comment that captures both the eccentricity of the quarter and the obliviousness of humans, a friend points out that all kinds of people live in the quarter—many dressed in the styles of their homeland. With luck they'd think she was "just another street entertainer with a great costume." So Jenny plunks a beret on her head, tucks her painting under her arm, and heads down Royal Street, blending in with ease. The fantasy is complete.

*Jenny quickly learned that, during the rush hours of traffic, she could run all of her errands. Grown-ups, as usual, were really too busy to notice the little giraffe. Racing to and from work, grown-ups were never aware that a little giraffe*

*was sharing the banquette, or sidewalk, with them . . .*
*maybe people thought that Jenny was just another one of*
*them.*

—*Cecilia Casrill Dartez,*
Jenny Giraffe Discovers the French Quarter, *1991*

Martin Charnin, lyricist and director of the musical *Annie*
as well as an avid giraffe fan, made a singing giraffe the star of
his 1976 children's book *The Giraffe Who Sounded Like Ol' Blue*
*Eyes.* Leon is a gifted crooner with a knack for "Strangers in
the Night" and "September Song." A crass agent turns Leon
down because he sounds "exactly like ol' Blue Eyes, y'know?
I'm sorry, kid." Years later the agent realizes his mistake, but
Leon now sounds like Neil Diamond.

Chuck Jones, who regularly suspended reality by creating Wile E. Coyote and other animated Warner Bros.
favorites, surrendered to the giraffe's seductive looks, its
silky grace, and its serene calm with the ultimate compli-
ment: the giraffe as sex symbol. His 1961 cartoon *Nelly's*
*Folly* stars a sultry singing giraffe from Africa whose stage
career is destroyed by her love affair with
a two-timing married male giraffe from
the local zoo. Snubbed by the public
and dismissed by her agent, Nelly
returns to the bush, where she finds
true love with a dapper spotted bari-
tone. The giraffes lived happily ever
after. The cartoon was nominated for
an Oscar.

Finally, the master of surrealism,
Salvador Dali, fully appreciated the
dreamworld quality of the giraffe.
The famed Spanish eccentric used

Original pencil
sketch of Nelly

the animal, engulfed in flames, to typify
his "search for impact and novelty,"
according to the founder of the Dali
museum. The "giraffe on fire" shows up
in a 1937 charcoal, a drawing of Harpo
Marx, and a 1937 oil painting (*The*
*Inventions of the Monsters*) and is believed

to have been inspired by René Magritte. Dali was so taken with the incongruity of the giraffe, he also began writing a script, called *Giraffes on Horseback Salad,* for the clown princes of absurdist comedy, the Marx Brothers. Alas, it was never filmed.

## The Giraffe as an Object of Awe and Mystery

The giraffe holds a prominent place in the folklore of the Hottentots, and one account of the origins of Kenya's Masai tribe says their name for God was *Em Ba,* or *Mba,* and they visualized His image as a Giraffe without horns. In southern Africa, the Kalahari San, a hunting-and-gathering people on the northwest fringe of the Kalahari desert, use a giraffe dance as part of their religious ceremony to produce the altered state of consciousness that leads to a transcendental mood and the ultimate protection and well-being of the group. The songs are named for strong things considered to possess healing energy.

Dr. John J. Kinahan, curator of the National Museum of Namibia, told me giraffes are so highly regarded in the vast, parched deserts of the region, they have been associated with rain. He relates the extensive paintings and carvings of giraffes there to religious ceremonies.

> *The belief of shamans, in southern African hunter-gatherer communities, that the spinal column serves as a conduit for ritual potency, might explain the evident importance of the giraffe in rock art of this region. Certain features of the species receive particular emphasis in this context. These include the pattern of body markings and the short upright mane. The variegated markings of the giraffe bring to mind the fractured vision associated with the onset of trance, while the erect mane evokes one of the common physical symptoms exhibited by dying game animals. As a visual clue for the peculiar rising sensation experienced by shamans during ritual trances, the giraffe would most likely have been of great interest and would have reinforced the animal's ritual importance.*
> —*John J. Kinahan, archaeologist, 1996*

One group of bushmen literally looked up to the giraffe by identifying it with the constellation of the Southern Cross. In the northern sky, the constellation Camelopardalis comprises a grouping of faint stars facing the Great Bear and next to Cassiopeia. But it takes a bit of imagination to fill in the lines, and it is considerably less visible than its earthbound relatives.

Several fiction writers understood the spell cast by the animal, as seen in this story by a little girl who falls in love with a zoo giraffe.

*She lifted her face and saw him, even taller than she had expected, his neck so long, his delicate nose held so high, that*

Giraffe "pecked" into Namibian shale, between 5000 and 1000 years ago

*a person could imagine him nibbling at stars. He walked very slowly, with a graceful forward lurch. He made no clouds of dust with his little elegant feet. Now it seemed to her that she had never known anything about a giraffe before. She had thought he would be spotted, brown on beige. Instead, his colors were laid upon him in fine, soft squares. The closer he came, the more she delighted in this coloring. It was as if his hide had been made in two layers, one creamy and pale, the other crisp and reddish brown. Maybe the dark upper layer had been too fragile for the equatorial heat. It had cracked into blocks, like the glaze on the Chinese pottery she had seen at Mrs. Moss's house. It had cracked, and the tan under layer was foaming through. Such a soft belly too, that creamy tan; and, flashing past her, moist with a dream of plentiful springs, two great brown eyes. . . .*

*"Oh, my darling, oh, my beautiful," she said. . . .*
*—Gladys Schmitt, "Consider the Giraffe," 1978*

Author Marie Nimier has written a dark, passionate tale about a man in love with a giraffe named Solange (based on the story of the real giraffe that walked to Paris—see chapter 7) including sexual fantasies and spiritual devotion that make for a most unusual fable:

*Solange might be nine feet tall, but she was still a small child, a shy, lost child like myself at her age. Our lives followed the same lines. No matter what I did, I was dependent on her, and she on me, we were bound together for life. . . .*

*I decided to try bottle-feeding her. The first few times, Solange seemed surprised to see me climb up the double ladder. It bothered her to have me suddenly reach her height. Wasn't her physical superiority her one and only privilege— a privilege of size? As if to show her displeasure, she chomped on the big rubber nipple I'd attached to a bottle, until I was afraid she'd swallow it and choke. However, when I offered her my fingers, she took them delicately in the groove of the tongue and the sucking reflex kicked in quite naturally. It gave me a strange pleasure.*
*—Marie Nimier, 1995*

## The Giraffe as Good and Pure, a Model of Virtue

In a legend of the Dorobo, a tribe in northern Kenya, the giraffe becomes the moral compass for two hunters, a sort of African Aesop's fable. It tells of a Dorobo hunter who yearned for a large, particularly elusive giraffe and enlisted a friend to help. When the friend fails to come through at the critical moment, the hunter decides to keep all the giraffe meat for himself. The friend is miffed and takes his revenge by tricking the hunter into loading his booty directly into his own hands. When the hunter realizes he has nothing left, he gets religion. The moral: He "realized that he had lost his whole giraffe owing to his selfishness."

One of the grandest myths to grow up around a giraffe originated in China. In 1414 Admiral Zheng He (Cheng Ho), the grand eunuch of the Three Treasures and the seafaring star of the Ming dynasty, sent an expedition to Bengal, where the ship's officers saw a giraffe that had been presented to the king. As the giraffe was unknown at the time in China, and no Chinese sailor had ever been to Africa, the men were amazed. They believed it to be a *ch'i-lin*, or *k'i-lin*, a mythological creature that appeared after Confucius' death and reappeared during the reign of a benevolent ruler. It was very good luck. The king of Bengal graciously offered his giraffe as a present to the emperor, and Zheng He arranged to have it shipped back home to China. Anxious officers, fearing that the strange beast might not make it, arranged for a second from the African city of Malindi a year

*The Giraffe Being Presented to the Emperor of China*, painted by Shen-tu on silk, 1415.

later. These were the first giraffes to reach the kingdom, and Emperor Cheng Tsu was enthralled. He was well aware that Confucian tradition considered the *k'i-lin* an auspicious omen, foretelling a reign of peace and prosperity, an abundant harvest and plenty of food. So when the second giraffe arrived in 1415, the emperor himself met it at the city gates. Throughout its life it was revered as the emblem of perfect virtue, perfect government, and perfect harmony, and the calligrapher Shen-tu inscribed a eulogy to the *k'i-lin* and to his ruler on a silk painting. First, the emperor:

> *I, Your servant, have heard that, when a Sage possesses the virtue of the utmost benevolence so that he illuminates the darkest places, then a K'i-lin appears. This shows that Your Majesty's virtue equals that of Heaven; its merciful blessings have spread far and wide so that its harmonious vapours have emanated a K'i-lin, as an endless bliss to the state for a myriad myriad years. I, Your servant, joining the throng, behold respectfully this omen of good fortune. . . .*
>
> *—Shen-tu, 1415*

Then, the giraffe:

> *Truly was produced a K'i-lin whose shape was high 15 feet,*
> *With the body of a deer and the tail of an ox, and a fleshy boneless horn,*
> *With luminous spots like a red cloud or a purple mist.*
> *Its hoofs do not tread on living beings and in its wanderings it carefully selects its ground.*
> *It walks in stately fashion and in its motion it observes a rhythm,*
> *Its harmonious voice sounds like a bell or a musical tube.*
> *Gentle is this animal that in all antiquity has been seen but once,*
> *The manifestation of its divine spirit rises up to Heaven's abode. . . .*

Another painting celebrates the same, or perhaps a later giraffe, on a long paper scroll.

*Auspicious clouds are facing the sun, and the prosperity of
the government is clearly in evidence.
The people will meet with great success, and there will be a
year of abundant harvest.
There will be plenty of food, and with songs they will praise
the great peace.*
                                                        —*Chinese poet, 1485*

The effect on the economy and on crop production are
not recorded, but the giraffe did inspire the first Chinese fleet
to sail to Africa, establishing the first Chinese African trade
links.  Giraffes became a favorite gift to the court throughout
the fifteenth century.

To some, the giraffe was not only magical, it was, with its
faraway look, its cool demeanor, its quiet manner, "cultured."
French naturalist André Thevet, quoting Italian poet Angelo
Poliziano, who'd composed some verses about Lorenzo de'
Medici's giraffe, was taken by the refinement of the beast he
saw in Cairo:

*This beast is the image of learned and educated people, as
Poliziano says; for they seem, at first sight, to be crude and
peevish, although by virtue of the knowledge they have they
are far more gracious, human, and affable than others who
have no knowledge whatever of sciences and virtue or who,
as is commonly said, have greeted the Muses only at the
threshold of the gate.*
                                                        —*André Thevet, 1554*

In World War II the giraffe took on an even more precious
symbolism:  the end of Nazi tyranny.  On the night of June 4,
1944, the secret message broadcast from London to the group
responsible for arming the French Resistance movement, was
"The giraffe has a long neck," a coded signal that D-Day was
twenty-four hours away.  In his book of the same name, Jacques
Poirier of the Special Operation Executive (SOE) told of hear-
ing those thrilling words on the BBC program "Ici Londres": It
meant he was to sabotage railway lines, destroy petrol dumps,
and disrupt enemy lines of communication.  "It informed me

that two days later we would emerge from the shadows, and that the dawn of freedom . . . was breaking at last."

Finally in this category, a giraffe symbol that goes beyond good luck to just plain good. The Giraffe Project was started in 1982 by Ann Medlock, who now runs it with her husband, John Graham, in Langley, Washington, a ferry ride from Seattle. They see the giraffe as a role model and use it to honor courageous humans who "stick their necks out for the common good"—people who make the world a better place. Some 850 "giraffes" have been identified so far, with no money, no prize, just a hearty recognition of their bravery. Among the honorees: a truck driver who blew the whistle on toxic chemicals in food carriers; two residents of the Bronx who developed a drug-free zone in their crime-ridden neighborhood; a minister in Montana who campaigns

**Stick Your Neck Out**

**The Giraffe Project**

against racial and ethnic discrimination; a woman in San Jose who feeds two hundred homeless people daily; and a ninety-eight-year-old woman from Seattle who campaigned for girls' rights in school sports at the age of twelve and hasn't stopped shaking up the system since. "Sometimes, sticking your neck out can really mess things up for you personally," Medlock says. "But we think there's a giraffe in every one of us, waiting to get out."

Why giraffes? I asked Medlock, whose project now encompasses a program for schoolchildren, a Web site, speeches, and TV plans. "Aside from the obvious verbal joke," she told me, "there are so many appropriate things about the giraffe: it has a huge heart, it can see things others can't, it's an herbivore, it doesn't hurt others, it's silent but not to be messed with."

"Have giraffes changed your life?" I asked.

"Oh, they ate my life."

"I say it every time ... 'Watch your he
Watch your head!' ... But do you li
Noooooo!"

ARSON

**Frank!**
**1? …**

# The Urban Giraffe

I t isn't easy being a giraffe in a world of man-made obstacles. At the turn of the century, East Africa's communications system was nearly wrecked by giraffes who tore down the telegraph wires newly strung around the countryside. Officials finally raised the lines above their horns and extendable tongues. Automobiles have proved a more lasting hazard, largely because the giraffe's eyes are so far above headlight range on Africa's unlit roads. And for every giraffe mowed down by a truck, it seems another has exacted revenge. They have smashed a car's radiator (with the hind legs), lashed out at the windshield (with the front legs), crushed the hood. They have been angered by near misses, by the toot of the horn, or, understandably, by the intrusion of the offending vehicles into their natural world.

But efforts to keep them out of African farmland—where they can cause expensive damage—have met with surprising ingenuity. Giraffes in the wild have learned to jump fences and to drink from the concrete troughs provided for cattle.

And giraffes uprooted from their tropical homes to live in northern climates have demonstrated a most efficient method of maintaining body heat: their hair grows longer in winter.

Their ability to accommodate modern civilization may be explained by their innate curiosity and friendliness. Giraffes just seem to like people and, with their peaceful nature, seem perfectly willing to let us share their planet while they explore what we've done to it. "It is a mild animal, does no mischief," correctly reported Buffon in his eighteenth-century *Natural History*. And it "may be conducted at pleasure by a small cord put round its head." Docility did not always serve them well. Just one hundred years ago photographer and hunter C. G. Schillings saw his first giraffes in the wild and "realised how thin and wretched our captive specimens are by the side of the splendid creatures of the velt." That is no longer true. Today zoo giraffes are healthy and vigorous, and while it would be the height of

**The modern zoo**

speculation to suggest that a wild creature with any sense might prefer a fenced yard to its natural home, the truth is, giraffes have thrived in captivity. Not only do they avoid the risk of being picked off by a lion or hyena, but zoo giraffes are well fed and generally better cared for—so much so that they tend to live longer than their kinfolk in the wild.

Modern zoos, with their emphasis on ecosystems and natural habitats, play a critical role in maintaining the world's animal populations, particularly endangered wildlife. They not only entertain and enlighten, they protect and preserve. "The wilderness is shrinking, the animals in it are on the way to extermination," observed one animal advocate recently, "and soon the only survivors will be those living in protected areas and zoos." The director of one of the nation's largest zoos points out that today there are *only* captive animals—whether in zoos, game parks, or sheltered sanctuaries. But they are no longer confined to private menageries designed to indulge wealthy monarchs.

The word "zoo," short for "zoological garden," was first used in the mid–nineteenth century, when Europe, then America, created animal parks for public enjoyment. The first to display giraffes was the Zoological Gardens in London's Regent's Park, which acquired three males and one female in 1836. They were also the first to mate in captivity, producing a calf on June 19, 1839. It lived only a few days, but a long line of subsequent offspring proved that breeding was successful beyond the wild.

The first giraffes to live in America resided in New York, initially at P. T. Barnum's American Museum, then at the old Central Park Menagerie in 1872. The first official zoo in America to display them was the Zoological Garden in Philadelphia in 1874. Four years later Cincinnati got a pair, but by 1925 there were reportedly only five giraffes in the entire United States. How come? The saga of the National Zoo in Washington, D.C., may explain.

In 1926 Dr. William Mann, the zoo's director, went abroad to obtain a wide variety of animals but ran into bad luck with giraffes in Tanganyika. The first calf they spotted got away, another kicked his way out of an overnight enclosure, and a third died of pneumonia in his packing crate ready for shipment. The demise of the captive had not yet been relayed to the folks back home when the Smithsonian telegraphed an impatient message: "Cable age, height, sex of giraffe, all particulars. School children in Washington holding contest to name it."

Uh-oh.

His credibility on the line, Dr. Mann stayed another month and purchased two Nubian giraffes from the game department in Sudan. He recounts the rest of the story:

*The pair was loaded at Port Sudan, and put first on one side of the promenade deck until the weather became cool in the middle of the Atlantic, when they were let down into the forward coal bunker. Having seen Mfaume drop dead, I had no confidence that I would have any luck bringing home giraffes. Each morning when I awoke, Saidi would be standing at the door with the latest news on their health. They were very sensible animals, and during some heavy seas we had they lay down in their crates and avoided the risk of breaking their necks or legs.*

*—Dr. William Mann, 1930*

The ship, also laden with a large leopard, green, blue, and purple monkeys, gnus, dik-diks, warthogs, and parrots arrived in Boston harbor in October 1926, an occasion of such moment, it was described by a breathless headline in the *Washington Herald*: 2,000 ANIMALS, 2 GIRAFFES ARRIVE FOR DC ZOO.

*Eventually they arrived in Washington, and we found that the school children had named them "Hi-Boy" and "Dot," and for a time they were Washington's leading citizens. Their arrival was the outstanding event in the history of the Zoological Park. A christening ceremony was held, in which the little boy and girl who had given the chosen names received their prizes, and all records for the number of visitors were broken during the next two months. . . .*

*We constructed a cage for them at one end of our bird house, where they had plenty of room to move about, and Mr. Blackburne, who during his thirty-eight years at the National Zoo had been without giraffes, stepped into the cage with them. He petted one, and received a vicious kick in his ribs. When he came out of the cage I asked him if the kick had hurt, but he replied, "No, it is a pleasure to be kicked by a giraffe in my own zoo."*

*—Dr. William Mann, 1930*

The pleasure didn't last. Within two years, kidney disease claimed first Hi-Boy, then Dot. Critics blamed their cramped enclosure, saying they should have had their own proper shel-ter, along with a runway and access to sunshine and fresh air. A newspaper columnist blamed the budget, not the zoo: "The officials did the best they could for the giraffes, but that best was not adequate." Dr. Mann told reporters the animals were too delicate and too expensive to replace.

For nearly a decade the nation's zoo had no giraffes, and it might have remained that way indefinitely without the persistence of a crusading newspaper editor. His name was Nicky Arundel and he was nine years old. From his home office in Wesley Heights, Nicky made the zoo's deficiency the lead editorial of his tiny tabloid neighborhood newspaper, *Nicky's News*.

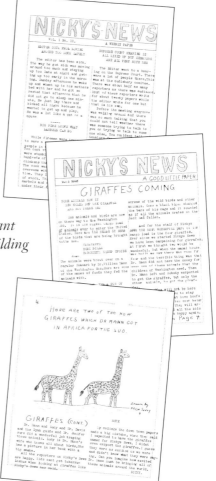

*The children of Washington want giraffes for the zoo. The new building is ready but the giraffes are still in Africa. Dr. Mann is in Sumatra and can get these giraffes if someone can send him the money. Every boy and girl in Washington should telephone the district Comishioners and ask about these giraffes. The Japanese children have giraffes. So do German and French children. Are they better than we are?*
—Nicky Arundel,
Nicky's News, *1937*

Nicky kept at it, renewing his call for giraffes in at least four subsequent issues.

*Somebody send the money quick.*
*If we don't get giraffes for the zoo then there cage wont do any good. If you have called the district comishioners and*

*they dont want to do anything about it why call the presi-*
*dent and may be he will get these animals.*

Luckily the prepubescent publisher had readers with the
right connections, as I learned when I telephoned him last
year. "Some congressman picked up the paper on his way to
work and read the editorial," recalled Arundel, whose Arcom
Publishing Company now owns a group of sixteen weekly
newspapers. "Then he slipped in an appropriation to fund the
purchase on some bill."

In 1937 the four new Nubians arrived, two males and two
females who had sailed through a monsoon and braved such
chilly temperatures in Halifax that handlers plugged in five
hundred-watt lamps to warm them. The giraffes were so fond
of the painted African landscape on their brand-new residence,
they tried to nibble its leaves. Clearly the National Zoo had
learned how to care for its new tenants, because the two pairs
ultimately bore a dozen living young. The nation's zoo has
never been without giraffes since.

As for our hero, one of the giraffes was named Nicky,
and he was featured in an article in *National Geographic*
magazine, complete with a photograph showing him seated,
editor style, at his typewriter. The young journalist celebrated his victory with jubilant headlines in the tabloid.

*BULLETIN!*
*THE GIRAFFES AT THE ZOO ARE ALL WELL. THEY LIKE*
*THEIR NEW HOME. DOCTOR MANN IS GOOD TO THEM.*
*End of Bulletin.*
                        —*Nicky Arundel*, Nicky's News, *1937*

Following his spotted success, Nicky also wrote editorials
against war and in favor of a new restaurant at the zoo. He got
the restaurant.

Today, obtaining a giraffe is a far simpler task, because
while they are valued up to $21,000 for a female (half as much
for a more rambunctious, neck-swinging male), most captive
animals are neither bought nor sold but bred in other zoos and
traded.

The zoo that has bred the most giraffes—the Mother of all Captive Giraffe Maternity Wards—is the Cheyenne Mountain Zoo (CMZ) of Colorado. Perched on a slope overlooking Colorado Springs, it calls itself "America's only mountain zoo" and is home to one of the largest giraffe herds in the nation—ten (as of this writing) reticulated beauties. Since 1954 CMZ has presided over 168 giraffe births—probably more, given the negligence of early record keeping. They've mastered the technique, keeping infant mortality down to only one calf death out of fifteen in the last five years.

In Colorado Springs, a giraffe entices visitors to the Cheyenne Mountain Zoo

General Curator Dale Leeds, whom I visited in December 1994, told me the zoo controls sexual contact carefully, letting the bull visit a cow in heat only when they want her bred. He also confirmed what I had learned about giraffe romance in the wild: that males prefer experienced, older females; that even in captivity, bulls butt their heads and swing their necks against other males to maintain the social hierarchy; and that giraffe sex is never recreational—only for breeding—with access strictly regulated by the female.

Leeds said they can tell when a female is pregnant when she stops coming into estrus, when she gains weight, and when they see movement in the abdomen—or the outline of a fetal hoofprint. But most cows' bellies don't show until they're halfway there, and one older, fatter female dropped her calf to the complete surprise of zookeepers. When they *can* tell, they remove the expectant mom about two weeks ahead of time to a special sanded stall, making sure another female is around to keep her company. Leeds pointed out that like most animals, giraffes give birth at night. The process usually takes an hour or so—five at the most—and if necessary, the keepers assist them "through the bars, because giraffe moms are so protective, they can be dangerous." Babies are standing within an hour and are kept inside at night to evade local mountain lions.

The cows, he went on, are excellent moms, "and if not, we do some training." For instance, he said, referring to his charges by name, "Rhonda rejected her baby, wouldn't nurse, so we put Rhonda in the chute—a kind of form-fitting stall, padded with dense foam and fitted out with support straps—and fed the baby with a bottle in the right nursing position;  all the while another person touched Rhonda to have her associate the act with good feeling." It worked. "Babies sometimes nurse with another mom," he went on. "Jane is like a brood mare—she'll let any other babies nurse with her.  She's had eleven of her own and is now—at age twenty-five—nursing two calves."

**Weighing a one week old at CMZ**

I asked how this very fertile center decided who got the new giraffes.  "All of our babies are spoken for," Leeds told me.  "Our policy is, if the zoo belongs to AZAA [the American Zoo and Aquarium Association, which accredits North American zoos], we're confident about their ethical standards," he said.  "If not, we go through a rigorous program of checks and balances—references and documents—to decide.  Then we make a recommendation to our Board of Directors."  CMZ has either sold, traded, or donated more than one hundred reticulated baby giraffes to zoos in the United States, Canada, and Mexico.

"I would never consider shipping a giraffe under six months," Leeds explained.  "I shoot for the one- to two-year level so I know they're stable.  I like to get it done before their second year because of the thirteen-foot overpasses on the highway!"  They used to place the animal in a crate, using a forklift, but then they had to worry that it wouldn't tip over.

Now they use the custom-designed chute, so someone from the receiving institution can drive right up and carry off the giraffe. To make sure the animal is comfortable, it will be acclimated to the chute for some days or weeks before the journey.

That is not the way it used to be done. The young giraffes that went to London in 1836 were captured in North Africa, sent by barge to Malta, and by steamer to London, then hiked to Regent's Park early one morning, led on leashes by two Nubian keepers in Abyssinian costumes. None of this fazed the globe-trotting animals. According to a magazine report, "their gentleness and docility were beyond expectation."

In 1993 a five-month-old, nine-foot-tall giraffe born in a Chicago zoo was sent to New Zealand in a heated crate with seven inches of headroom. He was escorted to the airport by a caravan of eleven cars and a truck; then, after an eight-hour delay in transit at New York's John F. Kennedy Airport, he flew twelve thousand miles without incident. The smooth journey was due in large part to the pilot, who took off and landed more gradually than normal in deference to the giraffe's sensitive circulatory system. By the time the giraffe arrived in Christchurch, he was, in the words of his keeper, "eating like a pig."

One of the more interesting journeys was related to me by Jack Stark, a former publicist for a now defunct zoo in Florida. In 1954 he helped transport a giraffe named Carol from New York City to Miami in an open-bed truck.

> *She was originally destined to be flown by air, but after measuring her height, it was found that she was too tall for any 1954 commercial aircraft—thus the trip by truck south. She left New York October 4 and arrived in Miami October 7, 1954. . . .*
>
> *I came along to work the rope since her head stuck up far above her canopy on the truck. My job was to ride in the back and pull her long neck down for the many cross-highway bridges that we drove under. New York papers went mad about it, and each night I had to phone up about her daily travels. They carrried a story daily until we reached Miami.*

*She caused quite a stir on the 1,300-mile trip south, with many waving motorists and kids: people would see her coming and almost drive off the road, and she made quite a fuss at a motel in Virginia, where we parked her outside on the lawn (staked her out), looking like a huge advertisement for the motel! . . . We had to duck stoplights as well as highway overpasses, and she went across the Maryland bridge, rode a ferry from Cape Charles to Norfolk, Va., and came down the New Jersey turnpike with its many overpasses. . . .*

*We had a great trip, and when we hit the Dade County line her fame had preceded her and we were met by TV and print media by the scores. She was a wonderful, young, patient giraffe, and we all fell somewhat in love with her on the trip. I often used to visit her later at the zoo and pet her. She was the zoo's first giraffe.*

*—Jack Stark, 1996*

Zoo stories from around the world have given me new regard for giraffe keepers. A bull giraffe at the Frankfurt zoo swung his neck at a pesky half-ton eland, propelling the antelope through the air and breaking its shoulder. A bull at the London zoo charged past its keeper and bashed a hole in the wall.

In the Calcutta zoo, one giraffe hanged himself when he stretched up for a leaf and got his neck stuck in a forked branch. And an ultra-sensitive female okapi from the Copenhagen zoo died at the age of five after hyperventilating from the stress of high-frequency sounds during a loudspeaker check at a nearby open-air

Carol gets used to her crate (top) and checks out a bridge in Maryland (right)

concert. In China, a zoo giraffe died after swallowing a plastic bag.

The main problem for giraffes in captivity is toenails. Out on the land, giraffes trim their hooves in the rocky or sandy earth. But their healthy diet and their limited need to travel in zoos allow hooves to grow out of control. "The problem is, the quick grows out with the claw," Dale Leeds of CMZ pointed out. That makes pedicures uncomfortable. CMZ lures the giraffe into the chute for paring.

Giraffes can be very fussy about their environment, probably a survival instinct for such vulnerable creatures. Every expert I talked to remarked on their sensitivity to change: "If the alarm goes off at six-fifteen rather than six, their day is shot," Leeds told me. "They like their routine." A paper bag in the yard will make them crazy.

At the Bronx Zoo, the largest in the nation and the pride of every New Yorker, keepers agreed that giraffes need to follow the same pattern all the time. "If you don't put them back in their stalls in the same order as always, it won't work," one said to me. "If you swing the gate the wrong way, you can get a blank stare. If somebody new tries to put them back, it can take an hour and forty-five minutes rather than thirty seconds!

**Bronx Zoo, 1906**

Anything different puts them off. They are extremely cautious—they worry when you change the hayrack. And if you don't pick up the trash in the public area by the pen, one of our females won't walk into the cage. She'll spot it immediately."

General curator Jim Doherty (thoughtfully wearing a giraffe tie) and senior wild animal keeper Kris Theis shared their wisdom about giraffes with me as we stood by the African plain,

**Clara oversees baby James IX, 1996**

where four fabulous female Rothschilds tore eagerly at the bark of a downed mulberry tree. They also reached down to munch on the grass, something giraffes were rumored never to do. From time to time one of them drifted over to the fence to check out nearby construction workers. Another played a reluctant game of tag with a pushy ostrich. Then it was back to the mulberry bark.

Doherty and Theis told me the fallen tree was a supplementary treat. Normally they eat alfalfa hay and multipurpose grain. Dale Leeds had noted that his giraffes eat "whenever they want. It's quite a human characteristic to eat beyond when you are full. Giraffes don't." I also learned that the Bronx babies lie down daily for a few hours at a time, but that Clara, who is twenty-one, never lies down; and that their eyelids droop but don't close. Clara's stamina has served her well. Two months after I saw her, she delivered her seventh calf— James IX, a strapping miniature of his proud parents.

Jim Doherty dismissed the idea that giraffes are mute. "Once we had a female giving birth, and something wasn't right with the baby. We tried to hand raise the calf, and when we put the mom into another stall she just roared. She was so unhappy." Dale Leeds had told me he heard a baby bleat, and a number of others have reported groans, snorts, moos, and even a bellow. One observer swears he heard a giraffe snore.

Zoo officials are understandably wary of when-did-you-stop-beating-your-animals questions, but I had to address the Victor issue: any problems with giraffes splaying? Giraffe lovers around the world had mourned another animal, just seven months after Victor's prominent demise. In April 1978 an eighteen-foot giraffe named Shlomo from the Tel Aviv Zoo slipped and fell to the ground. Ropes and pulleys were unsuccessful, and Shlomo succumbed. No such tragedies here, so far. The Bronx Zoo makes sure its herd breeds outside, where the footing is firmer. And here, as in Colorado Springs, the animals are not permitted outdoors when it's icy.

When there is a problem, animal experts deal with it openly. At the zoo in Santa Barbara, California, keepers have shown great sensitivity toward a female giraffe with—would you believe?—a crooked neck. The nine-year-old Rothschild developed the kink at the age of three, a zig that zagged more prominently over time. Noticing that neither her health nor her behavior seemed affected, and that the straight-necked giraffes and other animals treated her no differently, zoo officials decided she might provide an object lesson about disabilities. A sign by her enclosure now reads, "The young female giraffe has a neck deformity; we are aware of the problem and are monitoring it daily. She is in no discomfort. Thank you for your concern."

# CHAPTER TEN

# Where the Giraffes Are

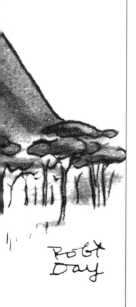

*Large game animals are disappearing so rapidly from Southern Africa that each year now sees the ancient limits of occurrence more and more circumscribed. . . .*

*In twenty years' time it may be safely said there will be very few Giraffes left, even in the inaccessible deserts where they yet seclude themselves.*

*— Henry Anderson Bryden, British hunter, 1891*

**F**ortunately for all of us, that dire prediction from a reformed hunter has not come to pass, thanks largely to a century of conservation and concern. Or at least, *more* concern. Giraffes are not now in danger of extinction, but the killings of the past combined with the development of the present means they will never again teem across the landscape by the hundreds in the great, graceful herds of ancient times. Perhaps it was their very abundance that led hunters and settlers and explorers to think they would have an unending supply of these mighty giants.

Or perhaps they didn't think at all. "In pre-colonial times the wild animals were not overexploited," concluded a United Nations panel in 1984. "There was no desire to eliminate them or even to domesticate them." Then came the settlers. The worst offenders were said to be the Boers of South Africa, who killed giraffes by the hundreds each year. The Boers were great marksmen. And deadly.

*Their creditable work of freeing South Africa of the dreaded lions, which roamed in such numbers that life was rendered unsafe anywhere in the country, is offset by their ruthless destruction of the giraffe from Cape Colony to the Botletli River. If they killed 6,000 lions in the Transvaal before existence was made safe, they may have killed 60,000 of the innocent, graceful giraffes. In the early days of South African history the giraffe was the most abundant game in the Transvaal, Matabel[el]and and Orange Free State, but the creature has been killed off like our American buffalo, and the few remaining representatives of a noble race gradually driven north. For years past the giraffe has been a profitable quarry for the Boer hunters, and the animal was valued by them only because the hides were articles of commercial use. They were pot-hunted, shot down in droves, and destroyed in the greatest number possible in every direction. The extinction of the animal in South Africa is now threatened, and its preservation by legislation comes when it is almost too late. In this respect, too, the brief history of the creature will resemble the story of our buffalo.*

*—G. E. W.*, Scientific American, *1899*

The Boers were not alone. Non-Africans of many nationalities literally took the lion's share of this splendid beast.

*For the extermination of the giraffe in the Transvaal, Bechwanaland, and the country immediately to the north of the Limpopo, Europeans are entirely responsible. The Boers killed most of them, of course, because up to 1890 Boer hunters were always in the proportion of at least ten to one*

*to white hunters of any other nationality. But, man for man, English hunters were quite as destructive. . . .*
*—Frederick C. Selous, hunter and conservationist,*
*1908*

By the turn of the century, the alarm had been sounded over and over and over:

*The death-knell of the giraffe has tolled. This wonderful and harmless animal is being completely annihilated. With sad, melancholy, wondering eyes the giraffe seems to peer into the world of the present, where there is room for it no longer. Whoever has seen the expression in those eyes, an expression which has been immortalised by poets in song and ballad for thousands of years, will not easily forget it. . . . The day cannot be far distant when the beautiful eyes of the last Twiga will close forever on the desert."*
*—C. G. Schillings, photographer and hunter, 1907*

*At the end of another century, our successors will probably, as they gaze at the pictures of the extinct camelopard, mar-vel that so extraordinary creature could have lingered so late into the world's history. Yet another hundred years and their successors will be inclined to rank the giraffe among dragons, unicorns, and other creations of fable.*
*—H. A. Bryden, British hunter, 1893*

*. . . these harmless and beautiful creatures—standing alone without allied living species, and but few extinct ones, and those doubtful—are upon the verge of utter extermination. . . . In fact, nothing will save these interesting animals from complete extermination but the strictest preservation from all shooting whatever for a term of years.*
*—Frederick V. Kirby, British hunter, 1896*

There was legislation, but to no avail in South Africa:

*For all practical purposes, the passing of the Game Law of 1892 was merely playing at legislation, a single £10 licence covering permission to kill giraffe, rhinoceros, eland, and*

*buffalo. That the three latter are nearly extinct now is a fact beside the question. Those who cannot find these animals will "take it out in giraffe," as I heard it remarked on one occasion. And as one good giraffe more than pays for the licence, the latter is indeed merely an incentive to slaughter—"We have to pay for them, so we'll kill them."*
*—Frederick V. Kirby, 1896*

By 1906 giraffes were among the rarest animals in South Africa, victims of the wholesale slaughter. A concurrent plague of rinderpest almost made them extinct. The East African giraffe population fared much better, largely because the Europeans and their guns got there so much later. In time, the importation of firearms enabled Africans to join the butchery. And countless do-gooders, in the name of science, contributed to the problem. One hunter helped exterminate giraffes, then asked to shoot the remaining animals so they could be stuffed for posterity.

Ironically, the closest thing to safekeeping was a stern ruler. In the north, it was said to be Muhammed Ahmed, the Mahdi of Sudan; in South Africa, Chief Khama of Bamang-wato, whose territory in Bechuanaland (now Botswana) included part of the north Kalahari desert:

*There the great chief carefully preserves the giraffes, and allows only his own people, or his own white friends, to kill them. The other point at which the giraffe country is still accessible to European hunters or naturalists is Somaliland, and the "unknown horn" of Africa. This district is so far accessible, that parties of English sportsmen yearly penetrate it from Berbera, making Aden their starting-point from British territory. But from the point of view of those who would delay as long as possible the extermination of the large game of Africa, the Dervish empire is not altogether matter for regret. No doubt the Arabs will still kill giraffes to make their shields from the hides, as they have done for centuries; but for the present the Soudan giraffes will be protected from raids like that in which those in the Kalahari Desert were destroyed in hundreds, because the price of "sjambok whips" had doubled. The Mahdi is, in fact, the involuntary protector of the wild animals of Central Africa. . . .*
*—London Spectator, 1892*

But with popular sentiment toward the animals starting to take hold, government attitudes began to change. Gradually they required licenses to shoot certain game; they officially discussed wildlife conservation in England; and in 1933 the London Convention on the Protection of the Fauna and Flora of Africa led to the formation of the national game parks.

Today wildlife laws protect most animals on government property, and one African country—Kenya— prohibits the hunting of giraffe (and all other animals) outright. Some African nations permit farmers to shoot giraffes without penalty, and some, including South Africa, Zimbabwe, Botswana, Namibia, and Tanzania, sell licenses to shoot giraffe. Fees and laws are determined nation by nation but seem to range from less than $50 to $5,000 or more. That doesn't include trophy charges, which can add another $1,000 or more. Professional hunters, who say proper licensing and strict ethics lead to good wildlife management, told me there isn't much demand for giraffes today. In South Africa, licensed hunters killed just eighteen in 1995, about the same number in 1996. Poachers, however, continue to menace many protected areas, and the demands of Africa's burgeoning population remain a constant threat to all wildlife.

No one knows the exact number, but the volunteer counters of the World Conservation Union estimate that some ninety-five thousand giraffes currently live in Africa. Add to that about one thousand in the world's major zoos, and an undetermined number in smaller facilities, and they just about equal the human population of Santa Barbara, California.

And just like humans, giraffes have gotten computerized. Starting in 1996, you could dial up the Internet and go to the Cheyenne Mountain Zoo's live Giraffe Cam—the only picture of a giraffe in cyberspace updated every three minutes.

But if you have the opportunity, I hope you will go to see them in Africa. Giraffes once flourished from Senegal to Somalia in the north, then all the way south to the Orange River. Now they have been pushed into a much more confined territory and are nearly extinct in the western countries. But you can readily observe them in most of the parks in eastern and southern Africa—and, of course, at Giraffe Manor in Nairobi.

On my first trip to Africa, the one that got me started on all this, I was introduced to the art of animal watching by a friend who had grown up in Kenya. She challenged me to get my "African eyes," which meant learning how to see the camouflaged shapes of the wildlife amid the unfamiliar jungle and bush. I was skeptical, assuming with big-city bravado that since I knew what an elephant and a leopard and, naturally, a giraffe looked like, I could spot them anywhere. I was wrong. I missed a herd of elephants in the Aberdare Mountains because they were covered with red mud and I was looking for gray. And I nearly neglected a lioness sleeping in a tree at Lake Manyara National Park because I didn't know to look up.

I do not mean to suggest that you need special training to spot a giraffe. But you will see it sooner, and it will be less frightened, if you spot the animal before it spots you. My first such success was in Samburu Game Reserve, a harsh desert area in Kenya's Northern Frontier District. As we rounded a curve, I spied a handsome reticulated giraffe out the side window of the car, nibbling the leaves from a tree just thirty feet away. We stopped the car and cut the motor before it moved, giving us precious seconds to watch and take pictures before the giraffe acknowledged our intrustion.

There's another reason to keep quiet, to listen and to look. Remember giraffe magic? It works.

*Despite their prominent markings and their enormous height, giraffes are not always easy to see. When one is looking about for game he is apt to watch for it near the ground, sweeping the landscape with his glasses and peering beneath the scattered trees. But with giraffes that method is very nearly hopeless. Somehow, even when one of these elongated creatures is standing behind only a single slender tree, it is very hard to make him out. I finally learned to look for their little heads and their big ears just above the tops of the trees upon which they feed. Many times I have been able to see a giraffe's head just above a table-topped acacia when I was utterly unable to make out his body and legs, even though the slender tree trunk did not hide him. Their long thin legs and their mottled bodies do not make a vivid picture, despite their coloring.*
*—James L. Clark, American naturalist, 1928*

Look for movement, look for shapes, and then sit back and smile.

When artist Eugène Delacroix visited the natural history collection in Paris that Tuesday in 1847, he acknowledged a "feeling of happiness" at seeing the animals in their museum setting—even the spindly stuffed version of the once celebrated star of Paris. "The further I went along, the more this feeling increased," he wrote in his journal. "It seemed to me that my being was rising above the commonplaces, the small ideas, the small anxieties of the moment." Reflecting on why the experience was so important, he concluded, "From the fact that I got out of my everyday ideas, which are my whole world, that I got out of my street, which is my universe . . . to give oneself a shaking up, to get one's head out . . . Certainly, seeing such things renders one better and calmer."

How much better and calmer, how far superior for one's head, when the animals are alive. Anna Merz, who has worked to save the African black rhinoceros from extinction, says, "If these go, we lose all our evolutionary potential—the splendor and the grandeur" of a treasured heritage. Giraffes aren't on the endangered list, but they nearly vanished once, and it's up to us to make sure they're never threatened again.

Of what use is a giraffe? I just like knowing it exists. Sure, I'm biased, but I can't imagine a world without tall blondes.

THE FAR SIDE      By GARY LARSON

"Uh-oh—did anyone remember to feed the giraffe tonight?"

# SELECTED BIBLIOGRAPHY

## Books

*Africa, the Art of a Continent.* New York: Guggenheim Museum,1996.

Africanus, Leo. *The History and Description of Africa and of the Notable Things Therein Contained.* Edited and Introduction by Dr. Robert Brown. London: Hakluyt Society, 1896.

Akeley, Mary L. Jobe. *Carl Akeley's Africa.* New York: Dodd, Mead & Co., 1929.

Albertus, Magnus, Saint. *De Animalibus. Book 22-26.* Translated by J. Scanlan. Binghampton, N.Y.: Medieval and Renaissance Texts and Studies, Center for Medieval and Renaissance Studies, 1987.

Alexander, Boyd. *From the Niger to the Nile.* New York: Longmans, Green & Co., 1907.

al-Jahiz, Amr ibn Bahr. *The Life and Works of Jahiz.* Translated by Charles Pellat. English translated by D. M. Hawke. Berkeley: University of California Press, 1969.

Andresch, Alfred. *The Night of the Giraffe and Other Stories.* Translated by Christa Armstrong. New York: Pantheon Books, 1964.

Baker, Sir Samuel W. *Wild Beasts and Their Ways.* London: MacMillan & Co., 1890.
———. *The Nile Tributaries of Abyssinia and the Sword Hunters of the Hamran Arabs.* London: MacMillan & Co., 1883.

Barnes, James. *Through Central Africa from Coast to Coast.* New York: D. Appleton & Co., 1915.

Barr, Cathrine. *Raffie.* New York: Henry Z. Walck, Inc., 1968.

Belon, Pierre. *Les Observations de Plusieurs Singularitez et Choses Memorables.* Paris: Benoist Preuost . . .Pour Gilles Corrozet & Guillaume Cauellat Libraries, 1553.

Bewick, Thomas. *General History of Quadrapeds: The figures Engraved upon wood by Thomas Berwick.* Newcastle-on-Tyner, 1820.

Blount, Margaret Joan. *Animal Land: The Creatures of Children's Fiction.* New York: Morrow, 1975.

Boorstin, Daniel J. *The Discoverers.* New York: Random House, 1983.

Bronson, Edgar Beecher. *In Closed Territory.* Chicago: A. C. McClurg & Co., 1910.

Bryden, H. A., ed. *Great and Small Game of Africa.* London: Rowland Ward, Ltd., 1899.

———. *Gun and Camera in Southern Africa.* London: Edward Stanford, 1893.

Buffon, Georges-Louis Leclerc, comte de. *Histoire Naturelle.* Various publication dates. Various publishers (some in his *Oeuvres Complètes*).

Cartmill, Matt. *A View to a Death in the Morning: Hunting and Nature Through History.* Cambridge, Mass.: Harvard University Press, 1993.

Charnin, Martin. *The Giraffe Who Sounded Like Ol' Blue Eyes.* Illustrated by Kate Draper. New York: E. P. Dutton & Co., Inc., 1976.

Ciardi, John. *Selected Poems.* Fayetteville: University of Arkansas Press, 1984.

Clark, James L. *Trails of the Hunted.* Boston: Little Brown, 1928.

Cosgrove, Stephen. *Memily.* Illustrated by Robin James. Los Angeles: Price Stern Sloan, 1995.

Crandall, Lee S. *The Management of Wild Mammals in Captivity.* Chicago: The University of Chicago Press, 1968.

Dagg, Anne Innis and J. Bristol Foster. *The Giraffe, Its Biology, Behavior, and Ecology.* New York: Van Nostrand Reinhold Company, 1976.

Damiri. *Ad Damiri's Hayat Al-Hayawan.* Translation by Lt. Col. A. S. G. Jayakar. London: Luzac and Co., 1908.

Dardaut, Gabriel. *Une Girafe pour le Roi.* Dumerchez-Naoum, 1985.

Dartez, Cecilia Casrill. *Jenny Giraffe Discovers the French Quarter.* Illustrated by Shelby Wilson. Gretna: Pelican Publishing Co., 1991.

Delacroix, Eugène. *The Journal of Eugène Delacroix.* Translated by Walter Pach. New York: Covici-Friede Publishers, 1937.

Dinesen, Isak. *Out of Africa.* New York: Random House, 1938.

————. *Shadows on the Grass.* New York: Random House, 1961.

Durrell, Gerald. *A Bevy of Beasts.* New York: Simon and Schuster, 1973.

Eliot, George. *Felix Holt, The Radical.* London: Penguin, 1987.

Estes, Richard Despard. *Behavior Guide to African Mammals.* Berkeley: University of California Press, 1991.

Farmer, Nancy. *The Warm Place.* New York: Orchard Books, 1995.

Galbraith, John Kenneth. *Ambassador's Journal.* Boston: Houghton Mifflin Co., 1969.

Gonzalcz de Clavijo, Ruy. *Narrative of the Embassy of Ruy Gonzalez de Clavijo to the Court of Timur at Samarcan, AD 1403-6.* Translated by Clements R. Markham. London: Printed by the *Hakluyt Society,* 1859.

Gordon-Cumming, Roualeyn. *Five Years of a Hunter's Life in the Far Interior of South Africa.* New York: Harper & Bros., 1850.

Gould, Stephen Jay. *Ever Since Darwin.* London: Penguin Books. 1991.

Grzimek, Bernhard. *Among Animals of Africa.* Translated by J. Maxwell Brownjohn. New York: Stein & Day, 1970.

Guggisberg, C. A. W. *Giraffes.* New York: Golden Press, 1969.

Hahn, Emily. *Zoos.* London: Secker & Warburg. 1967.

Hamsa, Bobbie. *Your Pet Giraffe*. Illustrated by Tom Dunnington. Chicago: Children's Press, 1982.

Harris, W. Cornwallis. *Portraits of the Game and Wild Animals of South Africa*. London: 1840.

———. *The Wild Sports of Southern Africa*. London: Pelham Richardson, 1844.

Heliodorus. *An Ethiopian Romance*. Translated by Sir Walter Lamb. London: J. M. Dent & Sons, 1961.

Himler, Ronald. *The Girl on the Yellow Giraffe*. New York: Harper & Row, 1976.

Hoberman, Mary Ann. *A Fine Fat Pig and other Animal Poems*. New York: Harper Collins, 1991.

Hoeffler, Paul L. *Africa Speaks: A Story of Adventure—Chronicle of the First Trans-African Journey by Motor Truck from Mombasa to Lagos*. Philadelphia: John C. Winston Co., 1931.

Hollis, A. C. *The Masai, Their Language and Folklore*. Oxford: The Clarendon Press, 1905.

Horace. *The Complete Works of Horace*. Edited and Introduction by Professor Casper J. Kraemer, Jr. New York: Random House Modern Library, 1936.

Hunt, John. *A World Full of Animals*. New York: David McKay Company, Inc., 1969.

Johnson, Robert Underwood. *Remembered Yesterdays*. Boston: Little, Brown and Company, 1923.

Johnson, Samuel. *Dictionary of the English Language*. London: Printed by W.Strahan for J. and P. Knapton, 1755.

Johnston, Sir Harry. *The Uganda Protectorate*. London: Hutchison and Co., 1902.

Kirby, Frederick Vaughan. *In Haunts of Wild Game*. London: Wm. Blackwood and Sons, 1896.

Kittenberger, Kalman. *Big Game Hunting and Collecting in East Africa—1903–1926*. London: Edward Arnold & Co., 1929.

Landucci, Luca. *A Florentine Diary from 1450-1516*. Translated by Alice de Rosen Jervis. New York: E. P. Dutton & Co., 1927.

Laufer, Berthold. *The Giraffe in History and Art*. Chicago: Field Museum of Natural History, 1928.

Lemaître, Pascal. *Emily the Giraffe*. New York: Hyperion Books for Children, 1993.

Leslie-Melville, Betty and Jock. *Raising Daisy Rothschild*. New York: Simon and Schuster, 1977.

LeVaillant, François. *New Travels into the Interior Parts of Africa by Way of the Cape of Good Hope in the Years 1783, 84 & 85 Volume II*. London: G. G. & J. Robinson, 1796.

Lhote, Henri. *The Search for the Tassili Frescoes*. Translation by Alan Houghton Broderick. New York: Dutton, 1959.

Livingston, Bernard. *Zoo Animals, People, Places*. New York: Arbor House, 1974.

Lloyd, Joan Barclay. *African Animals in Renaissance Literature and Art*. Oxford: Oxford University Press, 1971.

Loisel, Gustave. *Histoire des Ménageries de l'Antiquité à Nos Jours*. Paris: Octave Doin et Fils; Henri Laurens, 1912.

Madeira, Percy C. *Hunting in British East Africa*. Philadelphia: J. B. Lippincott Co., 1909.

Mandeville, John. *The Voyage and Travels of Sir John Maundeville*. London: Pickering & Chatto, 1887.

Mann, William M. *Wild Animals In and Out of the Zoo*. New York: Smithsonian Institution Series, Inc., 1930.

Maxwell, Marius. *Stalking Big Game with a Camera in Equatorial Africa*. London: William Heinemann Ltd., 1925.

Meyers, Norman. *The Long African Day*. New York: The Macmillan Company, 1972.

Morse, A. Reynolds. *Dali's Animal Crackers*. St. Petersburg, Fla.: Salvador Dali Museum, Inc., 1993.

Moryson, Fynes. *An Itinerary: Containing his Ten Yeares Travell Through the Twelve Dominions of Germany, Bohmerland, Sweitzerland, Netherland, Denmarke, Poland & Ireland*. Glasgow: James MacLehose and Sons, 1907.

Moss, Cynthia. *Portraits in the Wild*. Chicago: University of Chicago Press, 1982.

Nimier, Marie. *The Giraffe*. Translation by Mary Feeney. Kent, England: Angela Royal Publishing, 1995.

Oppian. *Works*. Translated by A. W. Mair. Cambridge, Mass.: Harvard University Press, 1987.

Patton, Willoughby. *The Florentine Giraffe*. New York: David McKay Co., 1967.

Pliny. *Natural History*. Translated by H. Rackham. Cambridge, Mass.: Harvard University Press, 1967.

Poirier, Jacques R. E. *The Giraffe Has a Long Neck*. Foreward by Jean Lesure, Translated by John Brownjohn. London: Leo Cooper, 1995.

Portmann, Adolf. *Animals as Social Beings*. Translation by Oliver Coburn. New York: Viking, 1961.

Purchas, Samuel. *Purchas His Pilgrimes: In Five Books*. London: Printed by William Stansby for Henrie Fetherston, 1625-6.

Reid, Captain Mayne. *The Giraffe Hunters*. Boston: Ticknor and Fields, 1867.

Riches, Judith. *Giraffes Have More Fun*. New York : Tambourine Books, 1992

Roosevelt, Theodore. *African Game Trails*. New York: Scribner's, 1910.

Sanderson, John. *The Travels of John Sanderson*. London: 1931.

Schillings, C. G. *In Wildest Africa*. London: Hutchison and Co., 1907.

———. *With Flashlight and Rifle*. London: Hutchison and Co., 1905.

Schmitt, Gladys. "Consider the Giraffe," *I Could be Mute, The Life and Works of Gladys Schmitt. Edited by Anita Brostoff.* Carnegie Series in English, New Series no.1, Pittsburgh: Carnegie-Mellon University Press, 1978.

Selous, Frederick Courtenay. *African Nature Notes and Reminiscences.* London: MacMillan & Co., Ltd., 1908.

Shepard, Paul and Barry Sanders. *The Sacred Paw.* New York: Penguin Books, 1985.

Silverstein, Shel. *A Giraffe and a Half.* New York: Harper and Row, 1964.

Smith, Bradley. *The Life of the Giraffe.* World Publishing Company, 1972.

Spinage, C. A. The Book of the Giraffe. London: Collins, 1968.

Stott, Ken, Jr., "The Incredible Giraffe," in *Strangest Creatures on Earth.* Edited by Edward M.Weyer, Jr. New York: Sheridan House, 1953.

Thevet, André. *Cosmographie de Levant.* Geneva: Droz, 1985. Reprint of original edition, published at Lyon: lan de Tournes et Guillaume Gazeau, 1556.

Topsell, Edward. *History of Four-footed Beasts and Serpents and Insects* (reprint of 1685 edition). New York: Da Capo Press, 1967.

Walker, Nick. *The Painted Hills: Rock Art of the Matopos.* Gweru: Mambo Press, 1996.

## Newspaper Articles and Periodicals

Brooks, Sydney, "Giraffe Hunting," *Harper's Weekly,* Oct. 2, 1897, 983.

Bryden, H. A. "On the Present Distribution of the Giraffe, South of the Zambesi, and on the Best Means of Securing Living Specimens for European Collections," *Proc. Zool. Soc. Lond.,* (1891): 445–47.

Carteret, Philip, "A Letter on a Camelopardalis Found about the Cape of Good Hope, from Capt. Carteret to Mathew Maty, M.D., Sec. RS," *Royal Society of London, Philosophical Transactions,* v. 60 (1770): 27–28.

Colbert, Edwin H. "The Giraffe and His Living Ancestor." *Natural History* (Jan. 1938): 46–50.

D'Aulaire, Emily and Ola D'Aulaire. "Above the Treetops, They Survey the World," *International Wildlife* (July 1974) 4: 28–31.

Foster, Bristol, "Africa's Gentle Giants," *National Geographic* (Sept. 1977): 402–21.

G. E. W., "The Boers and the Giraffe," *Scientific-American 81* (Oct. 21, 1899): 259.

Goodwin, George C. "Nature's Skyscrapers," *Animal Kingdom 59* (1956): 66–73.

Gould, Stephen Jay, "The Tallest Tale" in "This View of Life," *Natural History* (May 1996): 18–57.

Haweis, Stephen, "The Tall Twiga: A Giraffe with a Passion for Telegraph Wires," *Nature* (Feb. 1928): 106–8.

Jacobs, Jay. "Specialties de la Maison," *Gourmet* (August 1981):12.

Johnson, Mrs. Martin, "Toto-Twiga," *Good Housekeeping* (March 1930): 59, 242–43.

Lambourne, L. S., "A Giraffe for George IV," *Country Life* (Dec. 2, 1965): 1498–1502.

Langman, Vaughan A., "Giraffe Youngsters Need a Little Bit of Maternal Love," *Smithsonian Magazine* ( Jan. 1982): 95–103.

Langman, Vaughan A., O. S. Bamford and G. M. O. Maloiy, "Respiration and Metabolism in the Giraffe," *Resp. Phys.*, *50* (1982): 141–52.

Leuthold, Barbara M. and Walter Leuthold. "Food Habits of Giraffe in Tsavo National Park, Kenya," *East African Wildlife Journal, vol.10* (1972): 129–41.

Pratt, David M. and Virginia H. Anderson. "Population, Distribution and Behaviour of Giraffe in the Arusha National Park, Tanzania," *Journal of Natural History, 16* (1982): 481–89.

———. "Giraffe Social Behavior," *Journal of Natural History, 19* (1985): 771–81.

Rook, Jean, "Farewell, Dear Friend," *Daily Express* (Sept. 21, 1977).

Saint-Hilaire, Geoffroy, "Quelques Considérations sur la Girafe," *Annales de la Science Naturelle (Paris) 11* (1827): 210–35.

Stevens, Jane, "Familiar Strangers," *International Wildlife* (Jan./Feb. 1993): 11.

Van Citters, R. L., W. S. Kemper and D. L. Franklin, "Blood Pressure Responses of Wild Giraffes Studied by Radio Telemetry," *Science* (April 15, 1966): 384–86.